The
Kingore
Observation
Inventory

SECOND
EDITION

Bertie Kingore, Ph.D. AUTHOR
Jeffery Kingore GRAPHIC DESIGNER

PROFESSIONAL ASSOCIATES PUBLISHING

The Kingore Observation Inventory (KOI), 2nd ed.

Copyright 2001 Bertie Kingore
Third printing, 2004

PROFESSIONAL ASSOCIATES PUBLISHING
PO Box 28056
Austin, Texas 78755-8056
TOLL FREE PHONE/FAX: 866-335-1460
www.kingore.com

Printed in the United States of America
ISBN: 0-9657911-8-1

Contents

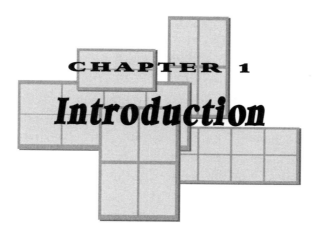

CHAPTER 1
Introduction

The Kingore Observation Inventory (KOI) is an instrument to assist educators in identifying and serving students with gifted potentials. It is the core of a system that encourages teachers to establish an enriched learning environment as it provides a structure to guide observation of the behaviors that gifted students typically exhibit in kindergarten through eighth grade. There are four major objectives of the KOI system:

1. To enrich classroom learning environments in order to uplift the level of thinking, production, and challenge for all students;
2. To assess all students' learning needs and responses so that the most appropriate levels and types of differentiation are immediately implemented;
3. To serve as one component in the identification of students for whom the regular curriculum is not sufficiently challenging and unlikely to promote high levels of learning, e.g., advanced and/or potentially gifted students; and
4. To provide a standard for teachers' analytical observations to document insights about their students to other educators.

One copy of the KOI is used for the entire class. A class observation instrument is important because the logistics of using individual instruments is overwhelming if a single teacher is expected to complete one for each student.

With the KOI system, each teacher organizes the observation and screening process as a series of opportunities for all students to demonstrate advanced behaviors. The intent is to be inclusive instead of exclusive by observing every student in a class and noting each student's response to a stimulating learning environment. Observing all children over a six-week period helps to identify students for whom additional identification data is merited. This intent is in the spirit of Tittle's (1979) "casting a wide net" so many able children are recognized for their potential and fewer able students settle for mediocre responses.

Being unable to see inside children's minds, educators can only gain insights into students' potentials from observation of their behavior and measurements of their performance. Standardized tests have long been a mainstay in identification of special populations.

Kingore, B. (2001). The Kingore Observation Inventory (KOI). 2nd ed. Austin: Professional Associates Publishing.

However, as Greenlaw and McIntosh caution, "Giftedness must be probed for in as many ways as it is manifested" (1988, p.88). Observation is a developmentally appropriate source of information for identifying gifted students (Karnes, 1983; Roedell, Jackson, & Robinson, 1980; Ross, 1993). Authentic assessment data is especially important to ensure identification of disadvantaged populations or under-represented students (Ford & Harris, 1999; Richert, 1997; Slocumb & Payne, 2000). While some argue that observation is too subjective, Renzulli reminds us that being subjective does not automatically mean being less appropriate. "If some degree of subjectivity cannot be tolerated, then our definition of giftedness and the resulting programs will logically be limited to abilities that can only be measured by objective tests" (Renzulli, 1978, p. 181).

Stimulating the learning environment and observing students' responses over a period of time is an important means of gathering information regarding students' strengths and needs. It enables educators to make decisions based on where a student's potentials may lead-- not on the opportunities the child has experienced in the past. It permits the consideration of behaviors and performance that are not assessable through the use of standardized tests (Ford & Harris, 1999; Karnes, 1983; Richert, 1997; Slocumb & Payne, 2000).

Thus, analytical observation through the KOI process enhances educators' understanding of the multiple facets of students' abilities and learning patterns. Dedicated teachers have often incorporated observations of learners in their assessments of needs and pacing. However, they felt limited in the usefulness of those informal observations when sharing their insights with other educators. Frequently, others' reactions signaled that it was only the teacher's opinion and therefore lacked a standard of validity.

Documentation of analytical observation is best accomplish through a combination of an anecdotal folder and a KOI folder. The anecdotal folder results in a collection of notes about every student's behaviors in learning situations so no student is overlooked. The KOI folder assesses students whose potentials extend beyond core-curriculum expectations. Using both folders ensures that the behaviors of all students are documented while not limiting the advanced potentials of some children. Procedures for an anecdotal folder are discussed on pages 7 and 8. Procedures for a KOI folder are elaborated in Chapter 2.

DEVELOPMENT & FIELD TESTING

The KOI evolved through ethnographic research over a 28-year period in hundreds of classrooms as the author worked with students in preschool through tenth grade, striving to help teachers identify and nurture advanced potentials. Although each gifted student is unique, many share characteristics that are observable. The goal was to structure defensible characteristics in a form that teachers could more easily use to increase their effectiveness in successfully identifying advanced potentials. The KOI is not designed to label students but to identify those with special talents and abilities needing differentiation beyond the regular curriculum. The goal was important because, as Karnes reflected, "Early identification and appropriate programming can foster habits and attitudes towards learning and toward the self that may prevent the gifted child from becoming an underachiever" (1983, p. 4).

Kingore, B. (2001). The Kingore Observation Inventory (KOI). 2nd ed. Austin: Professional Associates Publishing.

The KOI organizes characteristics of giftedness into seven categories: Advanced Language, Analytical Thinking, Meaning Motivation, Perceptive, Sense of Humor, Sensitivity, and Accelerated Learning. Page 5 provides a summary of each category. Negative behaviors associated with giftedness are correlated to the KOI categories on page 6.

Creative thinking and the most frequently-noted elements of creativity, i.e., fluency, flexibility, originality and elaboration (Torrance, 1984), are not listed as a separate category on the KOI because students may exemplify these elements in all categories. Creativity is revealed in students' use of language and word play, their original analytical thinking, their philosophy and search for meaning, their view of people and objects in the world, their delightful humor, and their sensitive responses. Creativity is subsumed--not isolated. Thus, students' creative responses will be integrated throughout the KOI. For some gifted students, creativity is demonstrated in how they go about doing something as well as in what they do.

After extensive informal use over a 15-year period, the KOI instrument was field test-ed and revised over a two-year period in 1987-1989. The characteristics and activities were initially field tested using children in a small number of classrooms. Characteristics and activities were revised or discarded, depending on the clarity of the communication to teach-ers and the ability to elicit a student behavior typical of giftedness. Then, a more ambitious evaluation was implemented with a larger and more representative sample of children involving 21 school districts in states located in the North, Northwest, South, and Midwest (kindergarten through third grade; total N=2793). The sample included Caucasian, Hispanic, Black, and Asian students whose socioeconomic status ranged from poverty level through upper-middle class. The initial edition of the KOI for primary grades was published in 1990. The initial construct validity study was published in 1993.

Numerous districts nationally and internationally have implemented the KOI sys-tem. Research data from 1990 through the present time is being compiled and analyzed by Dr. Karen B. Rogers at the University of St. Thomas. Those results, a construct validity study, and training materials to implement the system will be published in a KOI Training and Technical Manual (Contact Dr. Kingore or Dr. Rogers for more information.)

PHILOSOPHY OF THE KOI SYSTEM

Identification of gifted potential needs to focus on assessment that is ongoing and integrated with students' needs--rather than continue to mire in evaluation that only labels who is and is not gifted.

It is not the goal to label some students gifted and other students not gifted. The goal is to provide the most appropriate levels of instruction. However, research substantiates that high levels of instruction are more likely to occur in classrooms in which students' gifted potentials are identified.

Recognizing gifted potentials is not a reward for students. It is an awareness of needs so instruction can be differentiated to match readiness.

Kingore, B. (2001). The Kingore Observation Inventory (KOI). 2nd ed. Austin: Professional Associates Publishing.

Recognizing that some students have gifted potentials does not make them more important or more valuable. Every student is equally valuable by the nature of being human. Yet, every student is different, and many have dramatically diverse learning needs, rates of learning, and readiness levels. Having gifted potential means that students learn differently than others--not that they are better than others.

No matter how bright students may be, they are less likely to demonstrate advanced performance in any topic or content with which they have little or no experience. Therefore, enriching classroom learning environments for all students is a necessity if we truly seek to reach high potentials, particularly among under-represented populations.

All students deserve to learn at their highest levels of readiness--even the gifted.

LIMITATIONS OF THE KOI SYSTEM

1. The essential key to valid observational data is the training and attitude of the observers. Observers must understand the structure, objectives, and values of the observation process and the relevant behaviors to be noted. As Feldhusen asserts: "Teachers need special skills and understanding if they are to facilitate the personal, social, and academic development of talented youth" (1997, p. 547). The value of this process for the entire class must be accepted by the classroom teacher. Teachers are too busy to be bothered with any paperwork that does not clearly advance their instruction and benefit their students.

   Observation is best conducted by professionals who have continual contact with the students and who have been provided with quality in-service training that includes two components: 1. information regarding the nature and types of responses characteristic of students with gifted potentials, and 2. procedures for using the process effectively (Feldhusen, 1997; Roedell, Jackson & Robinson, 1980; Ross, 1993).

2. The ultimate goal of identification is to enable students to perform at their capacity. Thus, programs must be tailored to the needs of the students being served. The program should be stimulating, consistent with the student's stage of development, and compatible with the interests and abilities of the learner (Davis & Rimm, 1998; Greenlaw & McIntosh, 1988; Ross, 1993). Program developers need to have a vision of what gifted education should be and the difference it can make in the lives of gifted students.

3. Observation is but one piece of the identification puzzle. Multiple identification components must be integrated if an accurate view of the whole child is to emerge.

4. The open-ended activities and techniques shared in the KOI system are designed to be inclusive and implemented with all students. However, such activities do not constitute or substitute for a gifted differentiated curriculum. They are only starting points.

5. The activities and techniques shared in the KOI system may be similar to ones already used by good teachers. The main difference is an attitude of analyzing the behaviors and responses of all students as you observe for gifted potentials.

6. The process a student exhibits when learning may be as significant as the product. We must only evaluate a behavior or product as typical or atypical of gifted students if we observe the behavior or product in process.

Kingore, B. (2001). The Kingore Observation Inventory (KOI). 2nd ed. Austin: Professional Associates Publishing.

____ Categories of Gifted Characteristics ____

Advanced Language

The student unassumingly and appropriately displays an advanced vocabulary and an ability to effectively use more complex language in a variety of situations. The student naturally uses similes, metaphors, and analogies to express insights.

Analytical Thinking

The student demonstrates an ability to discern components of a whole, solves more difficult problems, and strives to determine more complex, abstract relationships and patterns in procedures, experiences, ideas, and/or objects. The student may not be appear organized yet enjoys organizing and planning events and procedures.

Meaning Motivation

The student exhibits an inner drive for thorough, independent understanding that results in the development of expertise in one or more areas. The student is philosophical, pursues issues atypical of agemates, demonstrates an extensive memory, and asks penetrating, intellectual questions.

Perspective

The student develops unique graphics or patterns and displays an ability to interpret and incorporate unexpected or unusual points of view through oral language, writing, manipulatives, art, and/or problem solving. The student insightfully interprets another's point of view.

Sense of Humor

The student demonstrates an appreciation of high levels of humor and an application of a finely developed sense of humor by understanding the subtle humor of others or by producing original jokes, puns, or other humorous effects. The student successfully uses humor to defuse volatile situations and gain approval.

Sensitivity

The student is very concerned about human issues, demonstrates a strong sense of justice, is intensely sensitive to the needs and motivations of others, and sets high standards for self and others. Empathy is expressed through words, art, or actions.

Accelerated Learning

The student demonstrates mastery or an ability to learn and interpret materials and concepts beyond the level typically expected for that age group. Exposure increases the rate of learning. The student ably uses a variety of tools to assess information beyond agemates.

Kingore, B. (2001). The Kingore Observation Inventory (KOI). 2nd ed. Austin: Professional Associates Publishing.

Negatively Perceived Characteristics
of the Gifted

    Students' behaviors can be perceived as positive or negative depending upon the situation and the observer. Richert stresses that the characteristics listed for teachers' ratings or observations should also include negative or unexpected characteristics indicated by the research (1982; 1997). Slocumb and Payne stress that the assessment of students from poverty requires the teacher to consider both the positive and negative manifestations of giftedness (2000).

    On the left side of the following figure is an adaptation of Richert's researched list of characteristics of the gifted that tend to screen them out of programs. On the right are the KOI categories associated with each characteristic.

CHARACTERISTICS	Advanced Language	Analytical Thinking	Meaning Motivation	Perspective	Sense of Humor	Sensitivity	Accelerated Learning
Bored with routine tasks		•	•				•
Refuses to do rote homework		•	•				•
Is more concerned with the concept than the details		•	•				•
Hands in messy work		•	•				•
Makes jokes or puns at inappropriate times	•				•		
Refuses to accept authority		•	•	•			•
Is nonconforming; stubborn		•		•			
Is reluctant to move to another topic			•				•
Overreacts					•	•	•
Gets angry or cries if things go wrong						•	
Domineers	•	•	•	•			
Disagrees vocally with others or with the teacher about ideas and values	•	•	•	•			
Is self-critical; impatient with failures		•				•	
Is critical of others or of the teacher		•	•				

Kingore, B. (2001). <u>The Kingore Observation Inventory (KOI)</u>. 2nd ed. Austin: Professional Associates Publishing.

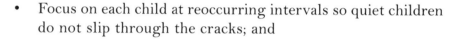

Anecdotal Folder

PURPOSE

The purpose of an anecdotal folder is to:

- Document observations of every child by systematically writing anecdotes to share with other educators and the parents;

- Increase the observer's understanding of the children's learning patterns and the multiple facets of their talents and potentials;

- Focus on each child at reoccurring intervals so quiet children do not slip through the cracks; and

- Accumulate a set of dated, specific anecdotes for each child that enhances the information shared at parent conferences and in report card narratives.

PROCEDURE

Begin with a brightly colored folder so it is easy to find on a busy teacher's desk. Decorate the outside if you wish, and use a marker to draw boxes inside--one for each child plus a couple of extra boxes for new children who arrive later in the year. If you enjoy using a computer, your decorations for the cover of the folder and the dividing lines for the inside can be drawn on your computer and then printed on a file folder ran through your printer. For large classes, or if you prefer more space to write notations, overlap two folders with the right half of one glued to the left side of the other in order to make a trifold providing three 8" x 11" areas.

1. Inside the folder, make each box the size of a Post-it Note™ so one note fits in each box. Use different sizes of Post-it Notes™ if you prefer to write longer notes about some children.

   OPTION: Glue a child's picture in each box, and write the name beneath the picture. The pictures may be photocopies of your class picture, photos from a digital camera, or a photograph you take of several children and then cut apart to separate the figures. The bonus with this folder is its usefulness for substitutes and special program personnel trying to associate children's names and faces.

2. Laminate the folder so it remains attractive and useful all year.

3. Set a goal to write continual records for each child, e.g.,one anecdote for each child every three weeks.

Kingore, B. (2001). The Kingore Observation Inventory (KOI). 2nd ed. Austin: Professional Associates Publishing.

4. Organize your folder by putting a blank Post-it Note™ in each box. Write the child's name or initials with the date on each note.

5. Observe and record anecdotes of your children's behaviors. After a few days, notice which children do not have an anecdote recorded, and strive to particularly observe them so you do not inadvertently miss a child.

6. As your observation period ends, move the completed anecdotes to each child's folder. Keep the notes in chronological order as you put them in the folder to increase their use over time.

WHAT DO YOU TRY TO OBSERVE?

- **Skill mastery**
  Which skills have specific children mastered? Which students require additional teaching or continued guided practice?

- **Skill integration**
  Are children appropriately applying the specific skills they have been taught?

- **Advanced behaviors**
  Which children consistently demonstrate responses that exceed expectations for this grade level?

- **Learning needs**
  Is a child frequently demonstrating behaviors typical of students with learning disabilities? Is additional assessment information recommended?

VALUES

An anecdotal folder is valuable when it enables teachers to:

- Ensure that the behaviors and needs of all students are observed on a regular basis;

- Document children's behaviors over time for narratives, report cards, and discussions with other educators or parents;

- Add depth to parent conferences through specific examples of behaviors and accomplishments (The parent will realize that you really know the child!);

- Document special-need assessments to provide information for more appropriate services for children with different learning and pacing needs; and

- Document KOI tallies.

Kingore, B. (2001). The Kingore Observation Inventory (KOI). 2nd ed. Austin: Professional Associates Publishing.

— The Value of Assessment and Identification —
Through Analytical Observation

THE KINGORE OBSERVATION INVENTORY ENCOURAGES TEACHERS TO BE "KID WATCHERS" WHO RESPOND TO AND EXTEND WHAT STUDENTS TRY TO DO.

To understand children, teachers must become analytical observers who seek to make sense of what they see occurring in learning situations. As teachers analyze behaviors, they frequently talk with students who have significant information to share when someone knows to ask. Talking with students about what they are doing provides a window to their thinking. Hence, teachers attempt to interpret and respond to what a child is trying to do by frequently questioning and probing for clarity. For example, when a young child scribbles or draws on a paper, interested teachers know to say to the child: "Tell me about your picture." The following are typical of other metacognitive prompts teachers use to probe student's thinking (Kingore, 1999a).

Reflective Questions
1. Tell me about your work.
2. What are you thinking about?
3. What did you do to begin this work?
4. Tell me more about that.
5. How did you figure that out?
6. Why do you think that is so?
7. What if this happened in a different order or sequence?
8. If this had not worked, what would you do?
9. How would you explain this to another student?
10. What evidence do you have to support that?
11. What changes could you make?
12. If needed, what would you do to gather more information?

THE KOI INCREASES TEACHERS' INSIGHTS ABOUT GIFTED POTENTIALS AS STUDENTS RESPOND AT MANY DIFFERENT LEVELS TO SIMILAR LEARNING EXPERIENCES.

Observation helps define and refine the students' levels of development and needs. The KOI categorizes the behaviors to watch for so teachers become aware of what gifted behaviors look and sound like. Analytical observation guides teachers to clarify their understanding of and appreciation for the differences among all wonderful children, i.e., average, high achievers, students with gifted potentials, and students with learning differences who may also demonstrate gifted potentials. As one primary teacher commented: "This gives me wonderful information about all of my kids. I'm noticing their strengths for a change instead of their deficits." A district coordinator commented that the KOI process is an ongoing inservice for teachers in interpreting students' needs and readiness levels.

Kingore, B. (2001). <u>The Kingore Observation Inventory (KOI)</u>. 2nd ed. Austin: Professional Associates Publishing.

THE KOI ALLOWS TEACHERS TO ASSESS THE PROCESS INVOLVED IN STUDENTS' LEARNING.

Tests and paper-and-pencil tasks customarily reveal what students get right or wrong. What may be equally important is information about how or why they go about developing those answers. For many students, the process is as significant as the product. For example, in one second grade classroom, the desks were arranged in a U-shape. As the teacher moved around the inside of the U to work with individual children, she noticed one of her boys had written his name upside-down. When asked about it, he replied: "I thought it would be easier for you to read as you walk by." His product, instead of being a directionality problem, indicated his awareness for viewing work from the teacher's perspective. Thus, his "error" was really one clue of advanced perspective typical of some children with gifted potential.

THE KOI PROCESS PROVIDES OPPORTUNITIES FOR MINORITY, ECONOMICALLY DISADVANTAGED, BILINGUAL, LEARNING-DISABLED, AND OTHER SPECIAL POPULATION STUDENTS TO EXHIBIT ADVANCED POTENTIALS.

One identification goal is to match the demographics of the districts population in all special programs. Special populations have historically been less represented in gifted programs partially because the identification process may have made it harder for them to reveal their abilities (Clark, 1997; Ford & Harris, 1999; Karnes, 1987; Slocumb & Payne, 2000). As the definition used in the Javits Gifted and Talented Education Act (1988) states, outstanding talents are present in children and youth from all cultural groups, across all economic strata, and in all areas of human endeavor. In the spirit of being inclusive instead of exclusive, it is helpful to think of the identification process as an ongoing series of opportunities given to all students in order to reveal potentials. This attitude is much more developmentally appropriate and sensitive to the background experiences of students than interpreting the screening process as a series of hurdles that students must successfully overcome.

Our challenge is to develop the talents of all students as we find and extend the potential of the more difficult-to-find gifted child. Because some children are not immediately able to demonstrate their future promise, the intent is to include all students in multiple classroom learning opportunities designed to elicit advanced potential and then observe how students respond. Slocumb and Payne admonish that schools cannot adequately assess ability without first providing opportunity (2000). One administrator reported:

> "Our star is a first-grade girl who was in a Chapter One classroom and spoke limited English. Through the KOI, a teacher picked up on her high potential despite her current lack of school-related background and skills. She was placed in our gifted program and within two years was one of our school's highest achieving students. We feel we could have missed her without the KOI."

Kingore, B. (2001). The Kingore Observation Inventory (KOI). 2nd ed. Austin: Professional Associates Publishing.

> *We can't change where students have been, but we can influence where they are going. Expend your energy providing opportunities for future learning successes. Set up your classroom with a wide array of challenging opportunities for all students and watch their responses.*

THE KOI INCREASES THE POSSIBILITY THAT THE IDENTIFICATION PROCESS IS USEFUL FOR THE ENTIRE CLASS AS TEACHERS OBSERVE STUDENTS AT WORK IN RICHLY CHALLENGING AND VARIED EDUCATIONAL SETTINGS.

Assessment and the identification process should not result in just a score to decide acceptance into a gifted program; it should be a process to provide helpful information to make instructional decisions for all students. To identify gifted attributes, effective teachers do not wait to see if such behaviors spontaneously occur. Rather, they set up high-level activities to engage the entire class. They choose learning experiences and strategies designed to be developmentally appropriate so all students can succeed, yet open-ended so students respond at different levels.

Multiple examples of enriched, open-ended opportunities for all student are presented in Chapters 6 and 7. With minimal preparation time, teachers can use these ideas to generate and lift children's thinking relative to any topic of study.

CONTINUAL USE OF THE KOI ASSESSES STUDENTS' POTENTIALS OVER AN EXTENDED PERIOD OF TIME.

All students do not blossom at the same time or in the same way. Late bloomers, quiet children, and students from special populations particularly need teachers' ongoing sensitivity to their emerging abilities. Therefore, the screening and identification process must evolve over a period of time to provide a sense of the student's development in response to learning opportunities. The gifted potentials of some students become known over time when enriched environments and nurturing professionals help them to blossom, develop a more positive self-concept, and approach their heretofore hidden potential.

Focusing on students' responses over a period of time provides a clearer view of potential than the proxy of student ability delivered through the snapshot of standardized tests. Rather than a one-time, checklist response, the KOI process encourages teachers to specifically consider the frequency and complexity of gifted behaviors over a length of time as they determine students' learning patterns. Differences in students' strengths and the multiple ways they exhibit potential become apparent as teachers analyze students' tallies on the KOI. A middle-school level teacher observed:

> "The KOI is very useful to me in searching for gifted potentials in secondary students. After using it for four weeks, I understand why longer observation is recommended. Kids do not always show high potentials in a few days. I am going to tally my classes all year."

Kingore, B. (2001). <u>The Kingore Observation Inventory (KOI)</u>. 2nd ed. Austin: Professional Associates Publishing.

CONTINUAL USE OF THE KOI DECREASES THE LIKELIHOOD THAT ASSESSMENT IS OVERLY INFLUENCED BY TEST-TAUGHT BEHAVIORS OR SPLINTER SKILLS.

Educators wonder if they are excessively aware of students demonstrating certain academic skills related to standardized tests. For example, when a young child is involved, a frequent concern is whether that child is truly gifted or just environmentally enriched and tutored by adults outside of school. The child might simply be demonstrating a test-taught behavior or a splinter skill--a skill such as the rote repetition of the alphabet taught out of context and without a solid concept base. Observation over a period of time provides numerous examples of students' responses to diverse learning opportunities. It usually becomes apparent if behaviors are consistent with advanced potentials or limited to a narrow and specific situation.

We want to encourage parents and others to provide as many enriching experiences as possible for children. As educators, our appropriate action is to respond to the needs and readiness level of each student. Incorporating appropriate levels of challenging content rather than too many cute, simple tasks provides a clearer vision of the potential of students.

THE KOI SIMPLIFIES THE TEACHER'S PAPER WORK AND INCREASES ACCURACY IN THE PROCESS OF ASSESSING STUDENTS WHO EXHIBIT OUTSTANDING TALENT OR PROMISE.

In the past, the most frequent procedure for collecting classroom information about gifted students required that teachers complete a checklist of characteristics. If we truly advocate seeking talents in all children, teachers would need to complete these checklists for every child. Filling out scaled checklists typically calls for extensive memory as well as analysis, evaluation, and decision-making on the part of the teacher. Past experiences suggest that the completion of these checklists is typically hurried and attempted in one intensive burst of activity the day before the results are due to the coordinator. Even the most dedicated teacher can be overwhelmed by the task of remembering and evaluating if and how much an individual child has exhibited each of the multiple characteristics. The practice of completing the KOI is sounder. Ongoing observation and tallying students' behaviors as they occur time improves a teacher's accuracy in recognizing and serving children with high potential. A fifth-grade teacher commented:

> "Analyzing kids by completing the KOI has certainly improved my observation skills. I am understanding more specifically the differences between high-achieving and gifted students."

THE KOI INTEGRATES WELL WITH OTHER ALTERNATIVE ASSESSMENT PROCESSES.

Observation complements the development and systematic selection of portfolio products and performance tasks useful in assessment, conferences, and talent development. Students' products selected over a period of time substantiate KOI tallies and enable other interested adults to view what gifted responses look like in natural learning environments.

Kingore, B. (2001). The Kingore Observation Inventory (KOI). 2nd ed. Austin: Professional Associates Publishing.

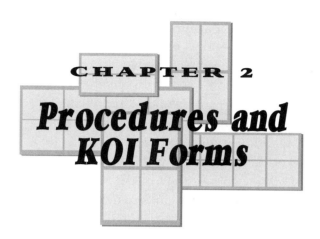

CHAPTER 2
Procedures and KOI Forms

PROCEDURES FOR USING THE KOI

1. Prepare a KOI folder.

Determine the level of the KOI that is applicable to your class. One level is appropriate for kindergarten through third grade; the second level is appropriate for grades four through eight. Both KOI levels are included in this chapter for you to copy and use with your class. Glue the two pages of the selected KOI inside a brightly colored folder; the colored folder makes it easier to find on your desk. Keep the KOI folder with your planning book for frequent reference and use.

2. Use one KOI for an entire class.

Just as a store manager takes an inventory of the store to determine what is needed, a teacher uses one observation form to assess all students' needs and instructional priorities. During any observation period, all the incidences of advanced behaviors in that class are recorded in one KOI folder. This procedure minimizes paper management and allows teachers to more readily analyze class patterns and needs.

Teachers who have multiple sections of classes typically mark tallies from all classes on the same KOI. If preferred, however, a teacher can certainly elect to use a different KOI form for each class section.

3. Mark behaviors that exceed grade-level expectations.

Record on the KOI only those behaviors that exceed the level and complexity typical for the age group. Noting students whose behaviors exceed grade-level expectations enables us to identify the students for whom the core curriculum does not promote the highest levels of learning.

The KOI categories include behaviors that most people may exhibit at one time or another. The difference between all students and the potentially gifted student is in the frequency, consistency, degree, and complexity of the behavior. Advanced students' behaviors exceed expectations for that grade level.

Kingore, B. (2001). The Kingore Observation Inventory (KOI). 2nd ed. Austin: Professional Associates Publishing.

4. **Record students' names in the category of the behavior.**

    When an advanced behavior is observed, determine the category for the behavior and write the name of the observed student in that area on the KOI form. It is not necessary to write the child's name beside a specific behavior. The listed behaviors in each category are there to illustrate examples of what that category involves.

    Each time a student demonstrates an advanced behavior in the same category, add a tally mark beside the student's name. Each time a student demonstrates an advanced behavior in another category, write the student's name in that area. Continue to tally each observed advanced behavior in the most appropriate category. Over time, these tallies reveal a pattern of the frequencies, consistencies, and categories of advanced behaviors for each child. Refer to the classroom examples in Chapter 3; they illustrate a KOI form after several weeks of observation.

5. **Observe for six weeks or longer.**

    A full range of advanced behaviors does not occur in one setting or in response to the same prompt. Thus, the KOI process is based on a minimum of six continuous weeks of analytical observation to identify more students whose responses exceed grade-level expectations.

    Developmentally, students' abilities emerge at varying times. Thus, ongoing observation may prove to be in the best interest of the children. For increased insight, many teachers continue recording behaviors on the KOI all year long. Every few weeks, switch the color of pen used to mark the tallies. The change in colors produces a simple, visual indication of when certain behaviors were marked. At the top of the KOI form, record the color and date for each observation period.

    In districts with a formal identification period, after that official period has ended, continue to observe and tally behaviors for your own information, and consequently, remain sensitive to the student whose abilities begin to emerge later in the year.

6. **Enrich the classroom environment to prompt advanced behaviors.**

    Advanced behaviors do not necessarily occur on demand. We would think it ludicrous if someone said to us: "I'm watching you. Do something gifted!" In the same spirit, dedicated teachers do not wait to see if gifted behaviors spontaneously occur during the course of learning. Rather, they choose many open-ended activities and strategies that allow all students to succeed while providing an opportunity for advanced students to demonstrate the highest levels at which they are able to respond. Teachers then observe and assess students' responses to these opportunities. This observation process encourages teachers to set up high-level, open-ended activities that benefit all students, observe the levels and complexity of their responses, and tally on the KOI those behaviors that exceed expectations.

> **Heat up the level of challenge in the classrooms**
> **and observe who bubbles up.**

Kingore, B. (2001). The Kingore Observation Inventory (KOI). 2nd ed. Austin: Professional Associates Publishing.

7. **Determine which category is the best fit for a behavior.**

Sometimes an observed behavior fits more than one category. For example, a student creates a complex metaphor (advanced language) that is also unexpectedly humorous (sense of humor). This dilemma is to be expected as all of these characteristics are integrated within the child. The characteristics are only isolated into categories to guide our understanding of what is observed. However, when an observed behavior seems to fit in multiple categories, tally it in the dominant category according to your first or strongest impression.

No single observation is to be tallied more than once. The reason for this practice emerged during field testing of the process. If a behavior could be marked in multiple categories, teachers pondered "what if" questions--"What if the student also meant...?" The process became time intensive instead of an on-the-run assessment. The patterns of students' strengths clouded as teachers struggled to mark a behavior in as many categories as possible. Thus, the appropriate teacher response is to mark a behavior in only one category. The KOI process encourages analysis over time and through multiple opportunities. If you use your professional judgment each time, a pattern of behaviors will emerge.

> ## One behavior = one tally

8. **Interpret the KOI results periodically.**

Analyze the results of your KOI observations periodically to provide valuable information about students' strengths and guide your instructional decisions. For example, if you have few tallies in analytical thinking, incorporate more challenging instructional activities in that category to ensure that ample opportunities are provided. Specific guidelines for interpreting observations are detailed in Chapter 3.

When you need to share your information with other educators, such as at the end of your district's six weeks observation period, complete the KOI Scoring Form in Chapter 3. The holistic rubric or your district norms are then used to interpret and quantify the data.

9. **Anticipate that only a few students exceed grade-level expectations.**

Since the KOI is used to record characteristics and behaviors that exceed grade-level expectations, it is probable that the names of most children in a class will not be recorded on the inventory. Furthermore, since few children are equally gifted in all areas, seldom does a child's name appear with equal frequency in each category. Most gifted children have tallies in three or four categories.

If you do not mark all students on the KOI, it does not suggest that you value those students less. Rather, it demonstrates that most students' learning needs are satisfied by the core curriculum. That is appropriate.

> ## If all students in the class show up on a KOI,
> ## either we do not understand what we are doing,
> ## or the core curriculum is totally inappropriate.

Kingore, B. (2001). The Kingore Observation Inventory (KOI). 2nd ed. Austin: Professional Associates Publishing.

10. **Interpret why some patterns emerge.**

Occasionally, a child has several tallies in only one category. The professional who best knows that child must interpret if that pattern indicates a single talent area in which to focus enrichment, or if the child's gifted potential requires multiple aspects of differentiation. Often, additional prompting, challenging learning experiences, and observation of student responses are required to reach a valid conclusion.

11. **Use the KOI as one component in a multi-criteria identification of gifted potential.**

The KOI is one component in an identification system. The behaviors of children provide educators with clues to interpret. Professionals avoid leaping to conclusions with information from only one source. No single instance determines who a child is, or is not, nor what that person most needs. Sound, educational decisions regarding the instructional needs of children result from the analysis of students' patterns of behaviors and the substantiation of that analysis with data from additional sources, such as student portfolios, information from parents, and test data.

> **Student responses and advanced behaviors provide clues, not conclusions.**

12. **Accelerated learning is only one of the ways to note gifted potentials.**

Some people identify gifted children by noting the learning skills they acquire early with greater ease. However, a word of caution is needed. Not all young children with gifted potential demonstrate accelerated learning at the beginning of kindergarten or first grade. Some children have not had sufficient exposure to literacy, math, or science experiences to demonstrate advanced levels of skills in academic areas. Furthermore, primary children may be gifted yet not demonstrate acceleration in many curriculum areas. Make every attempt to understand the child as a whole.

OPTIONAL PROCEDURES

1. **Mark the degree of the behavior.**

Some teachers prefer to indicate the degree of the behavior. When a behavior is particularly incredible, tally a plus sign (+) instead of the usual tally mark to help document outstanding responses.

2. **Support the tally with an anecdotal record.**

Occasionally, an anecdotal record of a particular experience is desired. The anecdotal folder discussed in Chapter 1 is an effective method to use. However, if an anecdotal folder is not used, carry a couple of peel-off address labels or Post-it™ Notes. When desired, quickly write a note, and at the end of the day, place each note inside a folder for that student. (Most elementary teachers report having a manila folder for each student in which they store "teacher stuff" they want to keep about that child.) The objective is that you do not have to recopy the anecdote or struggle to remember the incident at the end of your busy day.

Kingore, B. (2001). <u>The Kingore Observation Inventory (KOI)</u>. 2nd ed. Austin: Professional Associates Publishing.

— The Kingore Observation Inventory (KOI) —
Grades K through 3

TEACHER _____

SCHOOL _____ GRADE _____

Color	Date
❑	_____
❑	_____
❑	_____
❑	_____
❑	_____

ADVANCED LANGUAGE

Uses multisyllabic words unassumingly; descriptive

Asks questions about words (in print or oral language)

Uses similes, metaphors, or analogies; rich imagery

Modifies language for less mature children

Displays verbal skills when teaching others, handling conflicts, or influencing the behavior of others

Expresses similarities and differences

Uses the specific language of a discipline

ANALYTICAL THINKING

Demonstrates complex and abstract thinking

Analyzes classroom tasks and instructional techniques

Observes intensely; is unusually attentive to details in their environment

Takes apart and reassembles ideas, objects, or experiences

Analyzes cause and effect, consequences, or alternatives

Creates songs, stories, or riddles related to their learning experiences

Organizes collections or ideas in unique ways

MEANING MOTIVATION

Is philosophical; pursues issues atypical of agemates

Asks penetrating, intellectual questions; intense need to understand

Is curious; innovatively experiments

Remembers!

Displays an unexpected depth of knowledge in one or more areas; an "expert"

Demonstrates intense task commitment and energy when pursuing interests; persistent

Wants to do things independently

Synthesizes meaning through words, graphics, structures, or movement

Kingore, B. (2001). The Kingore Observation Inventory (KOI). 2nd ed. Austin: Professional Associates Publishing.

The Kingore Observation Inventory (KOI): Grades K through 3   **Page 2**

PERSPECTIVE

Interprets another's point of view

Demonstrates complex dimension or perspective in language, art, and problem solving

Creates and interprets more complex shapes, patterns, or graphics than agemates

Demonstrates that directionality is relative to position

Adds interesting components to enhance products

SENSE OF HUMOR

Says or does something indicating a sense of humor beyond agemates

Catches an adult's subtle or sophisticated humor

Uses figurative language for humorous effect

Understands and responds to the use of puns and riddles

Develops a humorous idea to the extreme; "flights of fantasy"

SENSITIVITY

Exhibits intense concern for human issues

Acts spontaneously to help someone in need

Shows nonverbal awareness of another's needs and feelings

Expresses empathy through words or art

Displays a strong sense of fairness and justice

Expresses high expectations of self and others; high-strung

Senses discord or dissatisfaction

Overreacts at times

ACCELERATED LEARNING

Requires minimum repetition for mastery

Increases rate of learning after introduction and exposure

Categorizes by multiple, often less-obvious, attributes

Comprehends symbolic representations, e.g., musical, numerical, alphabetical, mapping

Reads and interprets consecutive passages at an advanced level

Demonstrates an unexpected mastery of complex science or math concepts

Applies mathematical operations with sophisticated mastery

Creates advanced products

Accesses data with ease using an unexpected variety of tools

Kingore, B. (2001). The Kingore Observation Inventory (KOI). 2nd ed. Austin: Professional Associates Publishing.

— The **Kingore Observation Inventory** (KOI) —
Grades 4 through 8

TEACHER _____

SCHOOL _____ GRADE _____

Color	Date
☐	_____
☐	_____
☐	_____
☐	_____
☐	_____

ADVANCED LANGUAGE

Is verbally proficient; extensive vocabulary

Uses rich imagery; unusually descriptive

Uses similes, metaphors, or analogies to express insights

Modifies language for less experienced students

Displays verbal skills when teaching others, handling conflicts, or influencing others; persuasive

Expresses similarities and differences

Uses the precise language of a discipline

ANALYTICAL THINKING

Abstracts; conceptualizes; generalizes

Observes intensely; interprets observations

Thinks clearly, logically, and complexly

Thinks critically; may lead to skepticism

Recognizes relationships or patterns between diverse ideas or experiences

Enjoys analyzing and solving more difficult problems

Enjoys planning and organizing

MEANING MOTIVATION

Is philosophical; pursues issues atypical of agemates

Is curious; asks provocative, intellectual questions; innovatively experiments

Generates new ideas and unique solutions to problems; ingenious

Remembers; demonstrates extraordinary ability to process and retain information

Displays in-depth information in one or more advanced areas

Is intrinsically motivated to pursue areas of interest; intensely focused

Demonstrates heightened task commitment and energy when pursuing interests; persistent

Wants to do things independently

Kingore, B. (2001). The Kingore Observation Inventory (KOI). 2nd ed. Austin: Professional Associates Publishing.

The Kingore Observation Inventory (KOI): Grades 4 through 8 **Page 2**

PERSPECTIVE

Interprets another's point of view with insight
Demonstrates complex dimension or perspective in writing,
    oral discussions, art, or problem solving
Interprets past, present, and future ramifications
Develops unique graphic products or patterns
Incorporates interesting, subtle components to enhance products
Is attuned to the aesthetic characteristics of things

SENSE OF HUMOR

Says or does something indicating a sense of humor beyond
    agemates
Uses humor to gain approval or ease tension
Catches an adult's subtle or sophisticated humor
Displays intellectual playfulness; "plays" with language by
    using figurative language or puns for humorous effect
Uses humor that may be absurd or far-out
Develops a humorous idea to the extreme; "flights of fancy"

SENSITIVITY

Exhibits intense concern for human issues
Is intuitive and insightful of others' needs and feelings; inter-
    prets behaviors and counsels others
Cares deeply but may mask sensitivity
Expresses empathic statements through words or art
Bases friendships on similarity of interest rather than age
Displays concern for justice; seeks resolution of moral dilemmas
Organizes others to help promote change and fairness
Demonstrates high expectations of self and others; high-strung
Prefers solitude part of the time
Overreacts at times

ACCELERATED LEARNING

Requires minimum repetition for mastery
Exceeds the parameters of age-expected knowledge in a field
Creates advanced products
Creates or interprets symbolic representations
Reads above grade level with complex interpretations
Comprehends advanced ideas, concepts, or implications
Accesses data with ease using an unexpected variety of tools

Kingore, B. (2001). The Kingore Observation Inventory (KOI). 2nd ed. Austin: Professional Associates Publishing.

Explanation of Behaviors
CATEGORIZED IN THE
Kingore Observation Inventory (KOI)
• *Grades K through 3* •

ADVANCED LANGUAGE

Uses multisyllabic words unassumingly; descriptive

Gifted children who demonstrate advanced language are frequently noticed for their large vocabularies and unexpected use of multisyllabic words. For example, a child in second grade wrote a creative story about a rock music group which she named "Igneous". Because of their larger vocabularies, gifted primary children may also be unusually descriptive and use more adjectives than their age mates.

Asks questions about words (in print or oral language)

"What does that word mean?" "Why did you use that word?" Be especially aware of prereading four to six-year-old children who ask about the print on flaps, signs, and other words when an adult is reading a book to them.

Uses similes, metaphors, or analogies; rich imagery

These children incorporate more colorful language to express a point, such as a child who commented about all the pullout programs in the school: "Our school is like a hotel; people are checking in and out of here all day!"

Modifies language for less mature children

These children interpret and respond to the level of readiness of their audience. They may change the pitch of their voice as some adults do to talk with young children. Also, when talking to their less experienced peers, they may use less sophisticated words and shorter sentences.

Displays verbal skills when teaching others, handling conflicts, or influencing the behavior of others

These children become a mediator among friends. At times, they may referee disputes among classmates and try to help one child understand the viewpoint of another.

Expresses similarities and differences

These children may respond more readily, insightfully, and complexly when asked to compare seemingly unrelated objects, such as: "How is a pencil like a person?"

Uses the specific language of a discipline

Because of their larger vocabularies, these children integrate more specific science, social studies, and math terminology. If interested in writing, they are word collectors who particularly seek more interesting adjectives and verbs to use in their writing.

Kingore, B. (2001). The Kingore Observation Inventory (KOI). 2nd ed. Austin: Professional Associates Publishing.

ANALYTICAL THINKING

Demonstrates complex and abstract thinking
Gifted children who demonstrate advanced degrees of analytical thinking connect relationships that other children do not understand. They may form associations across time and disciplines as they study a topic.

Analyzes classroom tasks and instructional techniques
Primary gifted children like solving problems, such as figuring out how to improvise with common materials and objects. They may exhibit less trial-and-error behavior because they analyze the task before they begin.

Observes intensely; is unusually attentive to details in their environment
These children are highly observant and analyze what they see. Thus, they often get more out of a story, film, or field trip, and they are likely to retain information about what they observe.

Takes apart and reassembles ideas, objects, or experiences
"Let's take it apart and see what's wrong." These students frequently want to see what is inside an object and how it all works. They may display skills working new or different manipulatives because they analyze relationships as they handle parts of wholes.

Analyzes cause and effect, consequences, or alternatives
Unprompted, a student might comment: "That happened because..." or question: "What might happen if..."

Creates songs, stories, or riddles related to the learning experiences
Primary gifted children apply their learning through creative oral or written extensions of what they have learned. For example, they adapt a song shared in class by creating new words to fit the tune.

Organizes collections or ideas in unique ways
Many primary gifted children are collectors or organizers. They organize collections or data in unexpected or even insightful ways. They also like to organize other students: "You be the post office guy, and come to get my letter."

MEANING MOTIVATION

Is philosophical; pursues issues atypical of agemates
Young gifted children who exhibit advanced meaning motivation startle adults with their philosophical interests and questions, such as a kindergartner who said to her teacher: "If I only had my eyes and my brain, I would still be me because I could see things and think about them."

Kingore, B. (2001). The Kingore Observation Inventory (KOI). 2nd ed. Austin: Professional Associates Publishing.

Asks penetrating, intellectual questions; intense need to understand

These children ask unexpected, intellectual questions. They question and want to talk about things an adult does not expect them to even know. Their questions stem from their independent thinking and need for explanations.

Is curious; innovatively experiments

Most children ask questions pertaining to permissions, details, and functions. Gifted children ask questions motivated by intellectual curiosity rather than simple information gathering. They want to understand the reason or motivation behind an occurrence.

Remembers!

These children amaze adults with what they remember. They continue analyzing an issue until it makes sense, and then, they remember it longer.

Displays an unexpected depth of knowledge in one or more areas; an "expert"

Gifted children typically compile numerous details regarding subjects of interest. They may even clarify the answer of an adult or another student who uses less precise information, such as: "It's actually 365 1/4 days because..." These children become absorbed in one kind of knowledge or one area of specialization, and they may surprise adults with the depth of their information and concept mastery.

Demonstrates intense task commitment and energy when pursuing interests; persistent

When excited about what they are doing or learning, these students exceed the amount of time adults typically expect primary children to stay on a task. Their stimulated minds keep their bodies going.

Wants to do things independently

They prefer to go ahead with a project with a minimum of direct teaching. "I can do it." "Wait. Don't tell me. Let me figure it out."

Synthesizes meaning through words, graphics, structures, or movement

These students employ pictures, constructions, role playing, and verbalization to explain their meaningful interpretations.

PERSPECTIVE

Interprets another's point of view

Gifted children who demonstrate advanced perspective more readily understand another's viewpoint. They interpret what influences or motivates others. They may try to explain other viewpoints to peers or adults, such as: "What he meant was..."

Demonstrates complex dimension or perspective in language, art, or problem solving

The natural, artistic expressions of these students may reveal objects drawn from an unusual angle, such as a bird's eye view of a dog. Their conversations are filled with "but

Kingore, B. (2001). The Kingore Observation Inventory (KOI). 2nd ed. Austin: Professional Associates Publishing.

what about..." as they pursue the multiple perspectives of an issue. They frequently approach problems from atypical points of view.

Creates and interprets more complex shapes, patterns, or graphics than agemates

These children create amazing patterns with blocks, doodles, clay, tangrams, or graphics. Especially notice if their pattern is symmetrical or indicates more sophisticated planning.

Demonstrates that directionality is relative to position

These students understand the concept of left and right from multiple perspectives. When modeling the Hokey Pokey song, a first grader told the teacher: "You're doing it all wrong, but that's okay. The reason you're doing it wrong is because you're in front of us."

Adds interesting components to enhance products

More than just draw or construct to complete a project, these students add embellishments that enhance the total effect of the product.

SENSE OF HUMOR

Says or does something indicating a sense of humor beyond agemates

Gifted children who demonstrate advanced degrees of humor love to use it. When a story with layers of humor is read aloud, these children laugh at incidents and puns that peers do not understand.

Catches an adult's subtle or sophisticated humor

A gifted child frequently understands adults' jokes. One teacher commented about a boy who knew the other children did not understand her humor. So, each time she said something funny that went over the heads of the others, he just winked at her.

Uses figurative language for humorous effect

These children understand humorous language such as in The King Who Rained or the Amelia Bedelia books, and they make up new examples.

Understands and responds to the use of puns and riddles

Gifted students often comprehend the multiple meanings of a word and thus understand puns. They love to tell all kinds of silly jokes and frequently ask: "Do you get it?"

Develops a humorous idea to the extreme; "flights of fantasy"

To some adults, these students' humor may seem absurd, too silly, or go on too long.

SENSITIVITY

Exhibits intense concern for human issues

Gifted children who exhibit an intense degree of sensitivity seem to develop a concern for human needs and rights before their agemates. After seeing homeless people asleep on the street, a primary child asked his mother, "What is our family doing about this?"

Kingore, B. (2001). The Kingore Observation Inventory (KOI). 2nd ed. Austin: Professional Associates Publishing.

Acts spontaneously to help someone in need

Many gifted children are highly aware of others' needs. They may help another person without being asked.

Shows nonverbal awareness of another's needs and feelings

A young gifted child's face may reveal empathy for a character in a read-aloud story or for a peer in the classroom.

Expresses empathy through words or art

A second grader noted to a visitor: "Everyone expects Lisa to win so she's under more pressure than other kids." These children are capable of great empathy and insight into a situation.

Displays a strong sense of fairness and justice

These children insist that things must be fair. They exhibit an early interest in adult ethical issues such as prejudice and life's inequities. They often act against group pressures to follow through on what they perceive as right.

Expresses high expectations of self and others; high-strung

Gifted children may set high expectations for themselves and those significant to them. This is a negative behavior when it causes the child to shy away from new tasks or challenges in order to remain in control and always do well, i.e., perfectionistic behaviors.

Senses discord or dissatisfaction

Gifted children may be so attuned to the feelings and motivations of others that they intervene to counter a potential problem before help is requested. They exhibit a superior ability to interpret nonverbal clues.

Overreacts at times

The intense sensitivity of these children leads them to overreact, or seem to over-react, when perceived human needs are not met. Their reaction may seem excessive as they go on and on about an issue.

ACCELERATED LEARNING

Requires minimum repetition for mastery

Because many young gifted children need little repetition to master material, their learning accelerates. They are able to assimilate larger amounts of information and complex material more easily than average learners. They often master a new skill with unusual speed.

Increases rate of learning after introduction and exposure

Primary gifted children may exhibit substantial growth spurts in academic areas such as reading and math once learning begins.

Kingore, B. (2001). The Kingore Observation Inventory (KOI). 2nd ed. Austin: Professional Associates Publishing.

Categorizes by multiple, often less-obvious, attributes

Attribute listing and categorization are significant areas in which gifted students stand out. Especially note the degree of complexity of the attributes when a child simultaneously categorizes by more than one attribute, e.g., "These polygons are thin, red hexagons."

Comprehends symbolic representations, e.g., musical, numerical, alphabetical, mapping

Because of their analytical, observational, and meaning-oriented natures, these children understand and more readily incorporate symbols. They are often very interested in codes and ciphers.

Reads and interprets consecutive passages at an advanced level

Once these children make the reading connection, they usually move quickly into above-grade-level material. They are analytical and can relate more subtle inferences as they comprehend.

Demonstrates an unexpected mastery of complex science or math concepts

Math is an interesting area for gifted potentials to emerge because math talents are less influenced by cultural or language differences. A bilingual kindergartner asked his teacher: "Tell me about the numbers that come before zero. I know they call them 'negative'."

Applies mathematical operations with sophisticated mastery

These children more readily understand and explain the relationships of math operations. They enjoy manipulating multiple ways to work problems while classmates may only be ready to work on one operation such as addition or subtraction.

Creates advanced products

These students develop products that surprise adults with their complexity or concept density. Although the content is advanced, the product appearance may be either advanced or more simple, depending upon the strengths of the child.

Accesses data with ease using an unexpected variety of tools

Young gifted students are intrigued with reference materials at an earlier age and with more intensity than typical for their peers. They impress adults with the ease at which they use technology to access data.

Kingore, B. (2001). The Kingore Observation Inventory (KOI). 2nd ed. Austin: Professional Associates Publishing.

Explanation of Behaviors
CATEGORIZED IN THE
Kingore Observation Inventory (KOI)
• *Grades 4 through 8* •

ADVANCED LANGUAGE

Is verbally proficient; extensive vocabulary

Gifted students who demonstrate advanced language unassumingly incorporate multisyllabic words in their writings and conversations with adults and other able learners.

Uses rich imagery; unusually descriptive

Because of their larger vocabularies, these students frequently incorporate more extensive, richer descriptions. They are often highly elaborative in oral exchanges. Because of this elaboration, they may dominate more than their share of classroom discussions.

Uses similes, metaphors, or analogies to express insights

These students use more colorful language to express relationships. For example, a seventh grader attending summer classes for gifted students wrote in his evaluation of that program: "This program is an oasis on the desolate 'plain' of mediocre education."

Modifies language for less experienced students

These students are astute analyzers of the readiness level of others. They use less sophisticated words and simpler syntax when interacting with less experienced students.

Displays verbal skills when teaching others, handling conflicts, or influencing others; persuasive

Because gifted students can modify their language and frequently have extensive information, they can relate concepts in terms more readily understood by peers. A sixth-grade teacher said, "Tony helps me explain concepts to other students. When kids are really stuck, he's a better teacher than I am!" These students sometimes act as unsolicited referees during disputes among classmates and try to help them understand the viewpoint of others.

Expresses similarities and differences

Gifted students often respond insightfully, incorporate a more extensive information base, and associate seemingly unrelated objects. A fifth grader asked her teacher the meaning of "recalcitrant". When the teacher explained it meant to oppose or resist authority, the student commented, "Oh, it's like a mutiny. Have you read Mutiny on the Bounty? It's much more exciting than the old movie."

Uses the precise language of a discipline

As able students increase their concept mastery, they incorporate the more specific vocabulary of professional fields of study.

Kingore, B. (2001). The Kingore Observation Inventory (KOI). 2nd ed. Austin: Professional Associates Publishing.

ANALYTICAL THINKING

Abstracts; conceptualizes; generalizes
Gifted students who demonstrate advanced analytical thinking are able to make generalizations, more easily grasp the principles that underlie concepts, and apply them in other subject areas. Their ability to use complex associative methods provides an edge in science and math.

Observes intensely; interprets observations
These students are alert to their environment and continually analyze what they see. When content is not complex enough to engage them, they analyze the teacher's techniques.

Thinks clearly, logically, and complexly
Gifted students approach problems logically and are often confident of their reasoning ability, such as a sixth-grader who told his group, "Trust me. I know my answer is right."

Thinks critically; may lead to skepticism
John Holt in The Underachieving School refers to a student kept on campus to complete his work. Instead, he was creating a small printing press. In exasperation, Holt said, "If you'd just do the things you have to do... you could be free to do the things you want to do." With tired wisdom, the student replied, "No, you can't. They just give you more to do."

Recognizes relationships or patterns between diverse ideas or experiences
These students make mental connections between experiences or ideas. "That reminds me of when we..." They transfer learning to new situations.

Enjoys analyzing and solving more difficult problems
Gifted students thrive on and are stimulated by difficult problems. They particularly enjoy finding solutions to real-world problems as opposed to fantasy or contrived problems.

Enjoys planning and organizing
The collections of gifted students are typically complex and uniquely organized. Also, they enjoy planning the roles and processes for others. As a fourth grader noted, "I usually set up what a group will do because they know I can get it done right."

MEANING MOTIVATION

Is philosophical; pursues issues atypical of agemates
Students exhibiting advanced meaning motivation pose philosophical questions to adults whose opinion they respect. Their logic reflects high moral reasoning. Their questions stem from their independent thinking and need for explanation.

Is curious; asks provocative, intellectual questions; innovatively experiments
Gifted students' curiosity seems insatiable. They usually question not to annoy, but to probe why, rather than just what or how. They are "yeah-but-kids" who frequently respond with: "Yeah, but what about..."

Kingore, B. (2001). The Kingore Observation Inventory (KOI). 2nd ed. Austin: Professional Associates Publishing.

Generates new ideas and unique solutions to problems; ingenious

Gifted students generate large numbers of alternatives, such as a sixth grader who suggested changing several components of a board game to make it more challenging and interesting.

Remembers; demonstrates extraordinary ability to process and retain information

These students are capable of superior assimilation and marked retention. They startle adults with what they remember.

Displays in-depth information in one or more advanced areas

The range of gifted students' information is much more extensive than average. They exhibit concept density and may even correct another student or an adult who is incorrect or less specific. Their depth of information exceeds fact collecting to include interpreting patterns, future trends, and the unanswered questions of the areas of study.

Is intrinsically motivated to pursue areas of interest; intensely focused

These students pursue interests with intensity and concentrated energy. They occasionally may seem too focused in one area. These students exhibit interest in a wide range of specialized areas such as the development of new computer programs, political cartoons, ethics, or scientific research.

Demonstrates heightened task commitment and energy when pursuing interests; persistent

If they appreciate the task, these students are intrinsically motivated to stay on task until they think it is completed correctly. They like to use their creativity and inventiveness to embellish an assignment, such as an eighth grader who completed her research of ancient China's influence on Western development by writing on paper she had made.

Wants to do things independently

These students enjoy interactions with other students but also want to do things on their own. They may risk offering a differing opinion regardless of the group response. One eighth-grader proposed a correct, alternative process for an accelerated math problem and politely persisted defending the new process despite the disagreement of the class and teacher.

PERSPECTIVE

Interprets another's point of view with insight

Gifted students demonstrating advanced perspective frequently understand and reason from opposing points of view, such as: "For the Northerner that was true, but to a Southerner..." They interpret what influences the attitudes and opinions of others.

Demonstrates complex dimension or perspective in writing, oral discussions, art, or problem solving

These students' natural, artistic explorations produce objects or persons drawn from unusual angles or perspectives. When writing, they may employ more personification or create a story from a unique vantage point.

Kingore, B. (2001). <u>The Kingore Observation Inventory (KOI)</u>. 2nd ed. Austin: Professional Associates Publishing.

Interprets past, present, and future ramifications

Gifted learners associate relationships across time and from multiple perspectives. "How might a Native American living in this area 150 years ago react to our current proposal?"

Develops unique graphic products and patterns

The illustrations, graphic organizers, and patterns created by these students startle others with the complexity, intricacy, and sophistication relative to the age group.

Incorporates interesting, subtle components to enhance products

These students are more satisfied when creativity or inventiveness is incorporated in a situation or task. They adapt and improve ideas and products with unique perspectives.

Is attuned to the aesthetic characteristics of things

These students have aesthetic interests and are intrigued by the beauty of design and more complex, asymmetrical forms. During a problem solving competition, one sixth-grader demanded her group's sculpture "make sense, be operational, and be aesthetically pleasing."

SENSE OF HUMOR

Says or does something indicating a sense of humor beyond agemates

Gifted children who demonstrate a well-developed sense of humor love to use it in multiple situations. They see humor in more things because they see the bigger perspective of a situation.

Uses humor to gain approval or ease tension

These students may use humor to gain the attention and acceptance of their peers. They may even express a humorous perspective in a tense situation to relieve anxiety or defuse confrontation.

Catches an adult's subtle or sophisticated humor

Gifted students understand multiple layers of humor. They appreciate subtle humor often missed by other students. Also, they are quick to imitate the styles of humor currently popular with professional comedians.

Displays intellectual playfulness; "plays" with language by using figurative language or puns for humorous effect

These students enjoy exploring humorous alternatives and possibilities. They create new words for humorous effect and often enjoy multiple types of word play, including sniglets, hink pinks, and palindromes.

Uses humor that may be absurd or far-out

These students like to create humorous stories and jokes that seem far-out for their age. Since they comprehend multiple meanings of words, they use more puns and humorous forms that agemates do not understand.

Kingore, B. (2001). The Kingore Observation Inventory (KOI). 2nd ed. Austin: Professional Associates Publishing.

Develops a humorous idea to the extreme; "flights of fancy"

To some adults, these students' humor may seem to go too far or go on too long.

SENSITIVITY

Exhibits intense concern for human issues

Gifted students who exhibit an intense degree of sensitivity develop a concern for human needs and rights beyond the level of the general public.

Is intuitive and insightful of anothers' needs and feelings; interprets behaviors and counsels others

Many gifted students display intense sensitivity and intuition. They are alert to possibilities and have insight into the motives and feelings of others.

Cares deeply but may mask sensitivity

Gifted students' heightened self-awareness and awareness of others may intensify their preadolescent and adolescent feelings of being different. They vacilate between whether that difference makes them unique or just weird. At times, they experience an inner battle about how openly to express their feelings.

Expresses empathic statements through words or art

These students are capable of great insight and empathy. They verbally or graphically express sympathy for people's suffering.

Bases friendships on similarity of interest rather than age

Given their own choosing, many gifted students select older friends who have interests or mental abilities more similar to their own.

Displays concern for justice; seeks resolution of moral dilemmas

Gifted students may be idealistic and unusually sensitive to ethical issues of fairness, right, or wrong. It is difficult for them to compromise their views. They often act against group pressures and challenge authority when they perceive a situation to be unjust.

Organizes others to help promote change and fairness

The sensitivity of these students compels them to improve social conditions. They may expect others to help overcome injustices and right human wrongs. One fifth-grader organized a team of fourth through seventh grade students as volunteers to read aloud at a retirement home after learning that many senior citizens had vision problems.

Demonstrates high expectations of self and others; high-strung

Gifted students set high expectations for themselves and others significant to them. As one gifted teenager exclaimed, "'Gifted and talented' is not something you can take up lightly on free weekends. It's something that's going to affect everything about your life, twenty-four hours a day, 365 1/4 days a year" (Krueger, 1978, 141).

Kingore, B. (2001). The Kingore Observation Inventory (KOI). 2nd ed. Austin: Professional Associates Publishing.

Prefers solitude part of the time
As one seventh grader noted, "You can't work with others all the time without compromising what you really could do on a project."

Overreacts at times
The intense sensitivity of these students leads them to overreact, or seem to overreact, when perceived human needs are not met. They may go on and on about an issue.

ACCELERATED LEARNING

Requires minimum repetition for mastery
Because gifted students need little repetition to master material, their learning accelerates. They are able to assimilate larger amounts of information and more complex material in less time than average learners.

Exceeds the parameters of age-expected knowledge in a field
Gifted students generate ideas and information that seem significantly beyond expectations for their age. When planning a miniature golf course made from recyclable items, a fifth grader challenged the rest of the class by suggesting that the entire course be constructed to demonstrate principles of physics to other classes.

Creates advanced products
These students develop products that surprise adults with their complexity or concept density. Although the content is advanced, the product appearance may be advanced or more simple, depending upon the strengths of the child.

Creates or interprets symbolic representations
Because of their analytical, observational, and meaning-oriented natures, these students understand and readily incorporate symbols. They enjoy codes and more abstract, symbolic learning connections. Their ability to use complex associative methods often enables them to develop advanced expertise in science and math.

Reads above grade level with complex interpretations
If the environment and level of materials has provided sufficient challenge, the gifted may read two or more years above their grade level by the upper elementary grades. They frequently read and interpret near adult levels. Adults, who fear that gifted students may read material too advanced for them to truly understand, may be startled at the complex comprehension of which these students are capable.

Comprehends advanced ideas, concepts, or implications
Gifted students frequently understand implications that other students need to have pointed out for them. They operate at more abstract thinking levels most of the time.

Accesses data with ease using an unexpected variety of tools
These students are intrigued with reference materials at an earlier age and with more intensity than typical for their agemates. They readily use technology to access advanced levels of information.

Kingore, B. (2001). The Kingore Observation Inventory (KOI). 2nd ed. Austin: Professional Associates Publishing.

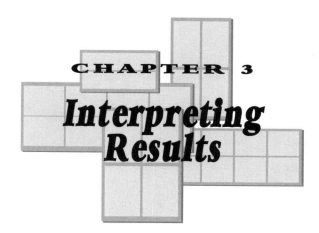

CHAPTER 3
Interpreting Results

Interpreting the results of KOI observations provides valuable information about students' strengths, needs, and potentials as it guides future classroom instruction. The KOI system encourages teachers to go beyond just determining which students are officially identified as gifted and which are not. Instead, teachers use KOI observations to differentiate instructional rates and levels in response to the needs of every student. Bright, high-achieving, or above-average students may also be present in your class in addition to potentially gifted children. Students who are not identified as gifted can still benefit from the more appropriate challenges you provide in your classroom. Teachers are empowered to differentiate instruction to serve all learners in their classrooms.

It is not the goal of the KOI system to label students. The goal is to serve the needs of all children in the most developmentally appropriate manner.

All students deserve to learn at their highest level of readiness-- even the gifted.

The National Research Center on the Gifted and Talented and Westburg's research (1993) document that differentiation of instruction beyond grade level is less likely to occur in classrooms unless students are identified as gifted. Therefore, the instructional reason to identify potentially gifted students is to determine children whose needs may not be met by the regular core curriculum.

This chapter presents two classroom examples of KOI observations to guide the interpretation process. The discussion of several points to ponder during an interpretation models that the analysis of students' behaviors in each classroom ultimately produces a greater value than just the quantifying of data through district norms or holistic scoring.

Expect many questions to occur when initiating a new process. Questions from teachers who have used the KOI are shared to help respond to the most commonly posed questions.

Kingore, B. (2001). The Kingore Observation Inventory (KOI). 2nd ed. Austin: Professional Associates Publishing.

Page 2

The Kingore Observation Inventory (KOI): Grades K through 3

PERSPECTIVE

- Interprets another's point of view
- Demonstrates complex dimension or perspective in language, art, and problem solving — Tyler |
- Creates and interprets more complex shapes, patterns, or graphics than agemates — George
- Demonstrates that directionality is relative to position — Cara ||\
- Adds interesting components to enhance products

SENSE OF HUMOR

- Says or does something indicating a sense of humor beyond agemates — Lynna
- Catches an adult's subtle or sophisticated humor
- Uses figurative language for humorous effect — George
- Understands and responds to the use of puns and riddles — Tyler |
- Develops a humorous idea to the extreme; "flights of fantasy"

SENSITIVITY

- Exhibits intense concern for human issues
- Acts spontaneously to help someone in need — Cara ||
- Shows nonverbal awareness of another's needs and feelings
- Expresses empathy through words or art
- Displays a strong sense of fairness and justice — Lynna |
- Expresses high expectations of self and others; high-strung
- Senses discord or dissatisfaction — Raul
- Overreacts at times

ACCELERATED LEARNING

- Requires minimum repetition for mastery
- Increases rate of learning after introduction and exposure — Lynna |||
- Categorizes by multiple, often less-obvious, attributes
- Comprehends symbolic representations, e.g., musical, numerical, alphabetical, mapping
- Reads and interprets consecutive passages at an advanced level
- Demonstrates an unexpected mastery of complex science or math concepts
- Applies mathematical operations with sophisticated mastery
- Creates advanced products
- Accesses data with ease using an unexpected variety of tools — Tyler ||

Kingore, B. (2001). The Kingore Observation Inventory (KOI). 2nd ed. Austin: Professional Associates Publishing.

The Kingore Observation Inventory (KOI) —
Grades K through 3

TEACHER _Ms. Wilhelm_

SCHOOL _Bryant Elem._ GRADE _2_

Color Date
■ _9-4 to 10-19_
☐
☐
☐

ADVANCED LANGUAGE

- Uses multisyllabic words unassumingly; descriptive — Darci |
- Asks questions about words (in print or oral language)
- Uses similes, metaphors, or analogies; rich imagery
- Modifies language for less mature children
- Displays verbal skills when teaching others, handling conflicts, or influencing the behavior of others — Tyler |
- Expresses similarities and differences
- Uses the specific language of a discipline

ANALYTICAL THINKING

- Demonstrates complex and abstract thinking
- Analyzes classroom tasks and instructional techniques — Raul |
- Observes intensely; is unusually attentive to details in their environment — Tyler |||\
- Takes apart and reassembles ideas, objects, or experiences
- Analyzes cause and effect, consequences, or alternatives — George |||
- Creates songs, stories, or riddles related to their learning experiences
- Organizes collections or ideas in unique ways — Catherine

MEANING MOTIVATION

- Is philosophical; pursues issues atypical of agemates
- Asks penetrating, intellectual questions; intense need to understand — Cara |
- Is curious; innovatively experiments
- Remembers!
- Displays an unexpected depth of knowledge in one or more areas; an "expert" — Darci |
- Demonstrates intense task commitment and energy when pursuing interests; persistent
- Wants to do things independently
- Synthesizes meaning through words, graphics, structures, or movement — Lynna ||

Kingore, B. (2001). The Kingore Observation Inventory (KOI). 2nd ed. Austin: Professional Associates Publishing.

Kingore, B. (2001). The Kingore Observation Inventory (KOI). 2nd ed. Austin: Professional Associates Publishing.

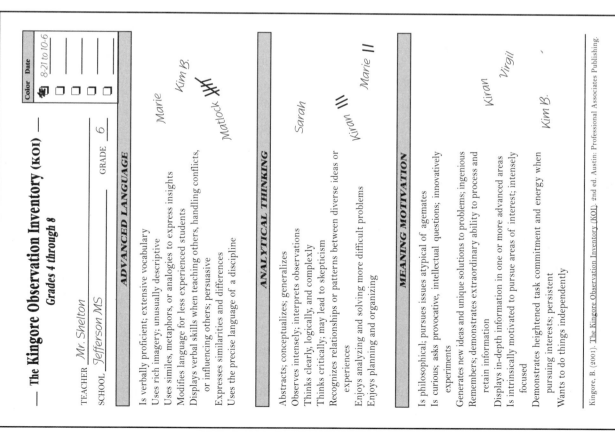

The Kingore Observation Inventory (KOI): Grades 4 through 8 Page 2

PERSPECTIVE

Interprets another's point of view with insight
Demonstrates complex dimension or perspective in writing, oral discussions, art, or problem solving   Virgil
Interprets past, present, and future ramifications
Develops unique graphic products or patterns   Kiran ||
Incorporates interesting, subtle components to enhance products
Is attuned to the aesthetic characteristics of things

SENSE OF HUMOR

Says or does something indicating a sense of humor beyond agemates
Uses humor to gain approval or ease tension
Catches an adult's subtle or sophisticated humor   Virgil |
Displays intellectual playfulness; "plays" with language by using figurative language or puns for humorous effect
Uses humor that may be absurd or far-out   Marie |V
Develops a humorous idea to the extreme; "flights of fancy"

SENSITIVITY

Exhibits intense concern for human issues
Is intuitive and insightful of others' needs and feelings; interprets behaviors and counsels others
Cares deeply but may mask sensitivity
Expresses empathic statements through words or art
Bases friendships on similarity of interest rather than age
Displays concern for justice; seeks resolution of moral dilemmas
Organizes others to help promote change and fairness
Demonstrates high expectations of self and others; high-strung
Prefers solitude part of the time
Overreacts at times

ACCELERATED LEARNING

Requires minimum repetition for mastery
Exceeds the parameters of age-expected knowledge in a field   Kiran |||| |
Creates advanced products
Creates or interprets symbolic representations
Reads above grade level with complex interpretations   Marie |
Comprehends advanced ideas, concepts, or implications
Accesses data with ease using an unexpected variety of tools

Kingore, B. (2001). The Kingore Observation Inventory (KOI). 2nd ed. Austin: Professional Associates Publishing.

The Kingore Observation Inventory (KOI) —
Grades 4 through 8

Color   Date
◼ 8-21 to 10-6
☐
☐
☐
☐

TEACHER Mr. Shelton
SCHOOL Jefferson MS   GRADE 6

ADVANCED LANGUAGE

Is verbally proficient; extensive vocabulary   Marie
Uses rich imagery; unusually descriptive
Uses similes, metaphors, or analogies to express insights   Kim B.
Modifies language for less experienced students
Displays verbal skills when teaching others, handling conflicts, or influencing others; persuasive   Matlock ||||
Expresses similarities and differences
Uses the precise language of a discipline

ANALYTICAL THINKING

Abstracts; conceptualizes; generalizes
Observes intensely; interprets observations   Sarah
Thinks clearly, logically, and complexly
Thinks critically; may lead to skepticism
Recognizes relationships or patterns between diverse ideas or experiences   Kiran |||
Enjoys analyzing and solving more difficult problems   Marie ||
Enjoys planning and organizing

MEANING MOTIVATION

Is philosophical; pursues issues atypical of agemates
Is curious; asks provocative, intellectual questions; innovatively experiments
Generates new ideas and unique solutions to problems; ingenious
Remembers; demonstrates extraordinary ability to process and retain information
Displays in-depth information in one or more advanced areas   Kiran
Is intrinsically motivated to pursue areas of interest; intensely focused   Virgil
Demonstrates heightened task commitment and energy when pursuing interests; persistent   Kim B.
Wants to do things independently

Kingore, B. (2001). The Kingore Observation Inventory (KOI). 2nd ed. Austin: Professional Associates Publishing.

Kingore, B. (2001). The Kingore Observation Inventory (KOI). 2nd ed. Austin: Professional Associates Publishing.

Points to Ponder:

Interpreting the Results of KOI Observations

INTERPRETING KOI EXAMPLES

After an appropriate period of observation, use the following questions to guide your analysis of the tallies marked on your KOI.

- How many of the class members were tallied?
- What are the number of tallies and different categories tallied for each student?
- When were specific behaviors tallied?
- Why do certain patterns emerge?
- What strengths and needs of the tallied students are suggested by these results?
- What are the instructional implications for the teacher?

The two classroom examples of the KOI forms in this section were completed over a six or seven week period of observation by teachers trained in the nature and needs of the gifted and in the KOI system.

Demographics of the example classrooms

THE PRIMARY EXAMPLE: Ms. Wilhelm's second grade class
- Socioeconomics: lower economic level; mobile area; 45% apartment dwellers
- Ethnicity: Caucasian 42%, Hispanic 33%, African-American 22%, Asian 2%, Native American 1%

THE MIDDLE SCHOOL EXAMPLE: Mr. Shelton's sixth grade class
- Socioeconomics: middle-class economic level; stable community; older, residential area
- Ethnicity: African-American 43%, Hispanic 28%, Caucasian 21%, Asian 8%

Number of students tallied

Compare the total number of children in these classes with the number who were tallied. Of the 29 students in the primary class, seven were tallied during the initial six week observation. Of the 31 students in the middle school class, six were tallied during the initial seven week observation. What does this imply? The students who were not tallied exhibited no observed responses beyond those expected for this age group. It is appropriate to anticipate that most students respond to learning experiences within the grade-level parameters.

All children are able to learn. All children benefit from enrichment, high expectations, and opportunities to engage in high levels of thinking. However, all children do not respond to the same prompts in an advanced manner.

Kingore, B. (2001). <u>The Kingore Observation Inventory (KOI)</u>. 2nd ed. Austin: Professional Associates Publishing.

Number of tallies and kinds of categories tallied for each student

Do not expect advanced students to demonstrate gifted potential in all seven categories. More typically, gifted children are tallied in three or four categories. These tallies provide clues to profile their talents and strengths as learners.

Students learn and excel in different ways. One value of the KOI is that it enables caring teachers to determine the pattern of strengths for each advanced learner. For example, children who are outgoing, confident, and verbal frequently demonstrate advanced language and sense of humor as two of their highest categories. In contrast, students who are shy, introspective, and quiet or students with limited English may exhibit the categories of analytical thinking, perspective, meaning motivation, or sensitivity; they are less frequently tallied in advanced language. Students who have benefited from enriched experiences are more likely to demonstrate accelerated learning as one of their high categories.

The KOI system challenges the educators who know the student best to analyze the pattern of strengths for each child tallied and appropriately match instruction to those needs. Thus, we can more effectively initiate differentiated services to those students in the classroom rather than just identify the gifted.

Remember to count each name as a tally. In the KOI process, the name is written the first time a behavior occurs; tallies are marked after that. When totalling the number of tallies for each student, add the tally marks to the number of times the name appears.

PRIMARY EXAMPLE

	TALLIES	CATEGORIES	ADVANCED LANGUAGE	ANALYTICAL THINKING	MEANING MOTIVATION	PERSPECTIVE	SENSE OF HUMOR	SENSITIVITY	ACCELERATED LEARNING
Tyler	13	5	•	•		•	•		•
Darci	4	2	•		•				
George	6	3		•		•	•		
Lynna	10	4			•		•	•	•
Catherine	1	1		•					
Raul	3	2		•				•	
Cara (ESL)	9	3			•	•		•	

MIDDLE SCHOOL EXAMPLE

	TALLIES	CATEGORIES	ADVANCED LANGUAGE	ANALYTICAL THINKING	MEANING MOTIVATION	PERSPECTIVE	SENSE OF HUMOR	SENSITIVITY	ACCELERATED LEARNING
Matlock	6	1	•						
Marie	10	4	•	•				•	•
Kim B.	2	2	•		•				
Sarah	1	1		•					
Kiran	15	4		•	•	•			•
Virgil	4	3			•	•		•	

Kingore, B. (2001). <u>The Kingore Observation Inventory (KOI)</u>. 2nd ed. Austin: Professional Associates Publishing.

When specific behaviors were tallied

The number of tallies is frequently not the only crucial factor. A trained educator must analyze the when or why of the tallies.

Teachers lack time to date everything tallied, yet the simple procedure of periodically changing the color of pen used to mark tallies enables teachers to determine generally when advanced behaviors occur. For example, clip a red pen on the KOI folder the first few weeks of observation; then, use a blue pen for the next few weeks, etc. Use the legend at the top of the KOI to record the colors and dates indicating when a tally occurred.

On the primary example, Darci received four tallies. However, the teacher, Ms. Wilhelm, reported that all of those behaviors were recorded in the last two weeks. The teacher is in the best position to use professional judgment and interpret what those responses suggest. One possibility is that Darci is a late bloomer or a less confident learner who is just beginning to respond to a safe, stimulating environment. If that is the implication, educators need to continue offering challenging opportunities and particularly watch her responses over the next few weeks to determine if a pattern of potentially gifted behaviors emerges. However, another possibility is that Darci loves the current topic of study. Again, the appropriate reaction is to continue to provide a stimulating learning environment and observe her responses. If her advanced responses are specific to just one topic, less advanced behaviors may be observed when different topics are studied.

On the sixth grade example, Virgil received four tallies in the last three weeks of the seven week observation period. Virgil has only attended this school for four weeks. The teacher, Mr. Shelton, plans to continue providing challenging experiences for Virgil and give him more time to reach his comfort zone in this class. The teacher believes that Virgil may emerge as one of the more advanced students. The records from his last school indicate that he was an A or B student in regular classes. Mr. Shelton believes Virgil can exceed that level and plans to challenge him with more complex content and higher expectations.

Why certain patterns emerge

Classroom teachers are often the most informed about their students and in the best position to use their professional judgment to analyze why a behavior occurred. Occasionally, when a student receives numerous tallies in only one category, the teacher needs to analyze why that atypical response occurred.

On the sixth grade example, Matlock has six tallies, but they are all in advanced language. An only child, Matlock is outgoing and typically one of the first to speak up in response to a class question or discussion. He was noticed for his verbal skills and nominated for a gifted program in a previous grade level. The sixth grade teacher concludes that Matlock is highly verbal and benefits from the attention encouraged by discussions, but that in all other categories, his behaviors are more typical for his age. Current portfolio products and last year's test data document the teacher's conclusion.

Kingore, B. (2001). The Kingore Observation Inventory (KOI). 2nd ed. Austin: Professional Associates Publishing.

When a student shows up with a significant number of tallies in only one category, that category is most often either accelerated learning or advanced language. Students such as Matlock, who are more frequently around adults or talked to with enriched vocabularies, may be observed only for their advanced language behaviors. As another example, some children from enriched home environments may be noticed for their accelerated learning behaviors because of the extended opportunities they have experienced and the content modeled at home. If a single category remains the only high behavior area for a student, the teacher provides enrichment and challenge in that area. However, educators need to continue observing responses to determine if a wider pattern of potentially gifted behaviors emerges with more time and exposure.

Strengths and needs of the tallied children

The KOI tallies signal a pattern of students' strengths and needs. Analyze the results of a KOI sample to determine the implied patterns of strengths for each tallied student. Cara, on the primary example, demonstrated a significant number of advanced behaviors in her class. An English as a Second Language student, her advanced responses tallied in meaning motivation, perspective, and sensitivity are indicative of her strengths. Since advanced language is measured in English, it is not surprising that she did not display advanced language behaviors at this time.

Marie, on the example with older students, is a shy person who seldom volunteers to share ideas and often acts as a loner during cooperative learning experiences. Some educators consider her immature because she does not interact. Her significant number of tallies on the KOI, however, reveal her strengths in analysis, sensitivity, and in-depth information and concepts.

Kiran is another student on the sixth grade example whose tallies clearly signal his strengths. He is a quiet student whose strengths are math and science. His four tallies in analytical thinking and seven tallies in accelerated learning reflect the complexity of his work in math problem solving and science concepts. In this class, his gifted behaviors are recognized and documented. He benefits from a differentiated curriculum.

Some patterns suggest above-average, high-achieving, or bright students instead of gifted potential. Analyzing these patterns might be useful to help other educators and parents understand the difference in the potential and needs of tallied students.

Instructional implications for the teacher

The behaviors marked on a KOI provide instructional implications for the teacher. A relatively small number of tallies can reveal patterns that increase our insight about students' talents and instructional needs. The KOI appropriately uses the professional judgment of trained teachers and other educators to assess students' behaviors for evidence of potential giftedness.

Kingore, B. (2001). The Kingore Observation Inventory (KOI). 2nd ed. Austin: Professional Associates Publishing.

On the two included classroom examples, the students who received few tallies demonstrated some advanced behaviors that signaled the teacher to continue providing challenges, prompt high-level responses, and observe their reactions. These initial behaviors suggest an above-average or high-achieving student rather than a gifted student. However, additional observations allow the possibility that these responses are just the tip of the iceberg for one or more students. Further challenge and observations could result in a more substantial pattern of gifted potential. Both teachers in these examples began using the KOI open-ended questioning prompts modeled in Chapter 5 to increase opportunities for high-level responses with each of their topics of study.

The students who received four to six tallies alerted the teacher to potential areas of strength for each child and signaled that these learners especially need challenge and faster pacing in one or more areas while further information is collected about their abilities.

The total number of behaviors tallied is relative to the opportunities provided in the class environment. The students who most frequently demonstrated gifted potential in these examples had nine to fifteen tallies. While test results and additional kinds of information were collected to document these children's potentials, the teacher began compacting the curriculum with these children in their areas of strengths, incorporating small group interactions to increase peer challenge, and using replacement activities with advanced content as appropriate to each student's readiness.

The KOI provides instructional feedback that benefits both teachers and children. Sometimes we provide less opportunities for high-level behaviors than we intend. Analyzing the KOI can provide a cross-check to meet our goal of prompting all categories of high-level behaviors as frequently and consistently as appropriate.

In the primary classroom, the teacher challenged herself to integrate more complex, high-level opportunities in language arts. Since oral and written language are such priorities for this age group, the teacher felt her class should have demonstrated more behaviors in advanced language. She concluded that she needs to ensure she is offering sufficient enriched content in that category. In the older class, the teacher marked no tallies in sense of humor. The teacher selected additional learning experiences that integrate with his curriculum and provide opportunity for humor. However, his inference is: because this class of students is more quiet and serious minded, less tallies in sense of humor are likely. Thus, as these brief analyses illustrate, the KOI helps teachers respond to students' potentials and provides feedback regarding the effectiveness of the high-level learning opportunities in the classroom.

COMPLETING THE KOI SCORING FORM

A blank KOI Scoring Form and two completed examples are included on pages 42 and 43. To complete the form, list the names, gender, and total tallies of the students who were recorded during observations. To indicate patterns of strengths, list in the Categories column the initials for each category in which each student received tallies, and add any comments that may be useful when interpreting students' needs. The following page explains how to complete the Holistic Score column.

Kingore, B. (2001). The Kingore Observation Inventory (KOI). 2nd ed. Austin: Professional Associates Publishing.

Holistic Scoring
of the KOI Observations

Since multiple-criteria identification is the national standard for determining gifted potential, the objective of Holistic Scoring of the KOI Observations is to reach a decision regarding the students for whom additional gifted assessment information is recommended. Using a holistic scoring strategy, the scorer takes all of the categories and criteria into consideration but aggregates them to make a single, overall quality judgment (Popham, 1997). The teachers or educators who have participated in the analytical observation process quantify their interpretations holistically and record them on a KOI Scoring Form. Many districts also use the holistic score as one criterion on the Student Profile (see pages 47 and 48).

Some districts use this rubric to assign holistic numerical values to each category and then total the results. This procedure is not recommended. A student scoring Above Average in all seven categories would have a higher total score (2 x 7 = 14) than a student scoring Very Superior in three categories (4 x 3 = 12). The procedure implies that students exhibiting behaviors in many categories are more advanced than students who consistently exhibit advanced behaviors in a few categories. This implication is not consistently valid. A student's gifted potential may be remarkable for the process, depth, complexity, and advanced level demonstrated in only a few categories. Students who have been exposed to fewer environmental enrichment opportunities are particularly likely to demonstrate remarkable behaviors in fewer categories (Slocumb & Payne, 2000).

RUBRIC			
1 **Average**	**2** **Above Average**	**3** **Superior**	**4** **Very Superior**
Typical; does not exceed the grade-level expectations Appropriate responses to the core curriculum standards	Strong, above-average responses on many tasks Occasional sparks of advanced potential Typical performance of high-achieving students	Consistent; exceeds standards and expectations of the grade-level Heightened abilities and insights Positive response to task complexity and challenge	Exceptional responses; substantially exceeds expectations Remarkable; strengths are clearly outstanding
Recommendation: Continued enrichment of the environment	**Recommendation:** Continued observation and challenge	**Recommendation:** Further assessment of gifted potential	**Recommendation:** Gifted identification with no reservations

If portfolios are not implemented as an assessment criterion to document students' gifted behaviors, growth, and achievements, teachers can elect to attach one to three classroom examples supporting their ratings of each student. These concrete examples enable others to understand the validity of teacher observations and insights.

Kingore, B. (2001). <u>The Kingore Observation Inventory (KOI)</u>. 2nd ed. Austin: Professional Associates Publishing.

KOI Scoring Form
Gifted Identification

District	District 57
School	Jefferson MS
Observation Period	8-21 to 10-6

TEACHER _Mr. Shelton_

GRADE _6_   NUMBER IN CLASS _31_

Student	Gender	Total Tallies	Categories	Holistic Score	Comments
1. Matlock	M	6	Adv.L	2	Challenge in Lang. Arts
2. Marie	F	10	Adv.L, AT, S, Acc.L	3	
3. Kim B.	F	2	Adv.L, MM	2	
4. Sarah	F	1	AT	1	
5. Kiran	M	15	AT, MM, P, Acc.L	4	Compact math & science
6. Virgil	M	4	MM, P, S	2	New-in district 3 weeks
7.					
8.					
9.					
10.					
11.					
12.					
13.					
14.					
15.					

1 Average	2 Above Average	3 Superior	4 Very Superior
Typical; does not exceed the grade-level expectations	Strong, above-average responses on many tasks	Consistent; exceeds standards and expectations of the grade-level	Exceptional responses; substantially exceeds expectations
Appropriate responses to the core curriculum standards	Occasional sparks of advanced potential	Heightened abilities and insights	Remarkable; strengths are clearly outstanding
	Typical performance of high-achieving students	Positive response to task complexity and challenge	
Recommendation: Continued enrichment of the environment	**Recommendation:** Continued observation and challenge	**Recommendation:** Further assessment of gifted potential	**Recommendation:** Gifted identification with no reservations

Kingore, B. (2001). The Kingore Observation Inventory (KOI). 2nd ed. Austin, TX: Professional Associates Publishing.

KOI Scoring Form
Gifted Identification

District	York Schools
School	Bryant Elem.
Observation Period	9-4 to 10-19

TEACHER _Ms. Wilhelm_

GRADE _2_   NUMBER IN CLASS _29_

Student	Gender	Total Tallies	Categories	Holistic Score	Comments
1. Tyler	M	13	Adv.L, AT, P, SH, Acc.L	4	Compacting math
2. Darci	F	4	Adv.L, MM	2	
3. George	M	6	AT, P, SH	2	
4. Lynna	F	10	MM, SH, S, Acc.L	3	
5. Catherine	F	1	AT	1	
6. Raul	M	3	AT, S	2	English Second Lang.
7. Cara	F	9	MM, P, S	3	English Second Lang.
8.					
9.					
10.					
11.					
12.					
13.					
14.					
15.					

1 Average	2 Above Average	3 Superior	4 Very Superior
Typical; does not exceed the grade-level expectations	Strong, above-average responses on many tasks	Consistent; exceeds standards and expectations of the grade-level	Exceptional responses; substantially exceeds expectations
Appropriate responses to the core curriculum standards	Occasional sparks of advanced potential	Heightened abilities and insights	Remarkable; strengths are clearly outstanding
	Typical performance of high-achieving students	Positive response to task complexity and challenge	
Recommendation: Continued enrichment of the environment	**Recommendation:** Continued observation and challenge	**Recommendation:** Further assessment of gifted potential	**Recommendation:** Gifted identification with no reservations

Kingore, B. (2001). The Kingore Observation Inventory (KOI). 2nd ed. Austin, TX: Professional Associates Publishing.

Kingore, B. (2001). <u>The Kingore Observation Inventory (KOI)</u>. 2nd ed. Austin: Professional Associates Publishing.

KOI Scoring Form
Gifted Identification

District

School

Observation Period

TEACHER _____

GRADE _____   NUMBER IN CLASS _____

Student	Gender	Total Tallies	Categories	Holistic Score	Comments
1.					
2.					
3.					
4.					
5.					
6.					
7.					
8.					
9.					
10.					
11.					
12.					
13.					
14.					
15.					

1 Average	2 Above Average	3 Superior	4 Very Superior
Typical; does not exceed the grade-level expectations Appropriate responses to the core curriculum standards	Strong, above-average responses on many tasks Occasional sparks of advanced potential Typical performance of high-achieving students	Consistent; exceeds standards and expectations of the grade-level Heightened abilities and insights Positive response to task complexity and challenge	Exceptional responses; substantially exceeds expectations Remarkable; strengths are clearly outstanding
Recommendation: Continued enrichment of the environment	**Recommendation:** Continued observation and challenge	**Recommendation:** Further assessment of gifted potential	**Recommendation:** Gifted identification with no reservations

Kingore, B. (2001). <u>The Kingore Observation Inventory (KOI)</u>. 2nd ed. Austin: Professional Associates Publishing.

Developing District Norms
for the Kingore Observation Inventory (KOI)

When assessing student behaviors for evidence of potential giftedness, each school district can develop its own norms as a valid reflection of the specific student population and professional judgment of the educators in the district. District norm data can be added to the Comments area of the KOI Scoring Form or substituted for the Holistic Score column. Norms are recomputed every year for the first three years and then every three years, thereafter. If the student population is large (500+ per grade), norms are established for each grade level.

Computer software is available for calculating statistics, or use the following procedure and form to determine district norms. A completed sample for determining district percentiles is included as one example. Percentiles are used because the majority of the districts in this project compiled data on a matrix or profile with percentile rankings, such as the Student Profile form and example in this chapter. However, computing standard scores and standard error of measurement is recommended to increase the confidence level of the interpretation. Procedures are in numerous statistical publications such as Robert Witte's in the References.

PROCEDURE

1. Determine the total population.

Add the number of students in each class to determine the total number of students (TNS) in the assessment. Record this number in the box at the top of the District Norms Form.

2. Record the number of tallies.

For each student listed on each KOI Scoring Form, make one mark on the District Norms Form in the row corresponding to the total number of tallies received.

3. Determine the frequency of each tally number.

Total the marks in each tally row to represent the frequency of students who received each number of tallies.

4. Calculate the Cumulative Frequencies.

Begin with the highest tally number, i.e., 15+ on the sample. Record the number of students who received that tally number in the Cumulative Frequency (CF) column. Then, add that CF to the number of students who received the next highest tally number to compute the next CF. The lowest tally number, i.e., zero, is the final CF and represents the total number of students.

5. Determine the percentiles.

Divide each CF by the TNS, and multiply the results by 100. Then, subtract this percentage from 100. Record the resulting percentile on the appropriate tally row in the percentile column.

EXAMPLE

$31 + 28 + 26 + 29 + 30 + 25 + 29 + 27 + 27 + 31 + 29 + 26 = 338$ total number of students evaluated (TNS)

(See the sample District Norms Form)

(See the sample District Norms Form)

From the sample District Evaluation Form:
- 15+ points (1 student) CF = 1
- 14 points (3 students) CF = 1+3 = 4
- 13 points (2 students) CF = 4+2 = 6

Continue, and calculate for all tally rows.

From the sample District Evaluation Form:
- 15+ points $[100-100(1/338)]$ = 99th %
- 14 points $[100-100(1/338)]$ = 99th %
- 13 points $[100-100(3/338)]$ = 98th %

Continue, and calculate for all tally rows.

Kingore, B. (2001). The Kingore Observation Inventory (KOI). 2nd ed. Austin: Professional Associates Publishing.

District Norms
FOR THE
Kingore Observation Inventory (KOI)

	Total Number of Students (TNS)
	338
	Observation Period
	9-15 to 11-6

DISTRICT _York Public Schools_   GRADE LEVEL(S) _K - 3_

Number of Tallies	Frequency (Number of Students per Number of Tallies)	Total Frequency	Cumulative Frequency (CF) *Add from bottom up*	Percentile $100 - \left(\dfrac{100 \, CF}{TNS}\right)$	Number of Tallies
0	266	266	338	*Average or below*	0
1	JHT JHT IIII	14	72	79	1
2	JHT JHT III	13	58	83	2
3	JHT IIII	9	45	87	3
4	JHT III	8	36	89	4
5	IIII	4	28	92	5
6	JHT I	6	24	93	6
7	JHT	5	18	95	7
8	II	2	13	96	8
9		0	11	97	9
10	III	3	11	97	10
11	II	2	8	98	11
12		0	6	98	12
13	II	2	6	98	13
14	III	3	4	99	14
15+	I	1	1	99	15+

Kingore, B. (2001). <u>The Kingore Observation Inventory (KOI)</u>. 2nd ed. Austin: Professional Associates Publishing.

District Norms
FOR THE
Kingore Observation Inventory (KOI)

Total Number of Students (TNS)
Observation Period

DISTRICT _____   GRADE LEVEL(S) _____

Number of Tallies	Frequency (Number of Students per Number of Tallies)	Total Frequency	Cumulative Frequency (CF) *Add from bottom up*	Percentile $100 - \left(\dfrac{100\ CF}{TNS} \right)$	Number of Tallies
0					0
1					1
2					2
3					3
4					4
5					5
6					6
7					7
8					8
9					9
10					10
11					11
12					12
13					13
14					14
15+					15+

Kingore, B. (2001). The Kingore Observation Inventory (KOI). 2nd ed. Austin: Professional Associates Publishing.

Student Profile:
Gifted Identification

	District
	York Schools
	School
	Bryant Elem.
	Identification Period
	9-4 to 10-19

NAME __*Cara*__   GRADE __*2*__

BIRTHDATE __*6-12-93*__   AGE: (YEARS) __*7*__ (MONTHS) __*3*__

COMMENTS _____

__*English Second Language*__

__*Used highest indicator on CTBS*__

_____

HOLISTIC SCORE:	1	2	3	4
PERCENTILE				
2	16	50	84	98	99.9
-2SD	-1SD	MEAN	+1SD	+2SD	+3SD

1. __*Kingore Observation*__
   __*Inventory--Superior*__
   __*(District norm: 97%)*__

2. __*Comprehensive Test of Basic Skills*__
   __*Total Lang.: 84%; Math: 95%*__
   __*Total Battery: 91%*__

3. __*WISC-3*__
   __*129*__

4. __*Portfolio*__
   __*10 / 12*__
   __*94%*__

5. __*Parent Information Form*__
   __*3*__

ACTION PLAN __*Committee*__
__*recommends placement in gifted*__
__*program.*__

Average   Above Average   Superior   Very Superior

24%   76%   92%   98%

Kingore, B. (2001). <u>The Kingore Observation Inventory (KOI)</u>. 2nd ed. Austin: Professional Associates Publishing.

Student Profile:
Gifted Identification

	District
	School
	Identification Period

NAME _____   GRADE _____

BIRTHDATE _____   AGE: (YEARS) _____ (MONTHS) _____

COMMENTS _____

_____

_____

_____

HOLISTIC SCORE:	1	2	3	4		
PERCENTILE						
2	16	50	84	98	99.9	
-2SD	-1SD	MEAN	+1SD	+2SD	+3SD	

1. _____

_____

_____

2. _____

_____

_____

3. _____

_____

_____

4. _____

_____

_____

5. _____

_____

_____

ACTION PLAN _____

_____

_____

_____

Average   Above Average   Superior   Very Superior

24%   76%   92%   98%

Kingore, B. (2001). The Kingore Observation Inventory (KOI). 2nd ed. Austin: Professional Associates Publishing.

Questions from Teachers
Using the KOI

How can I be sure in what category to place a tally?

Know the seven categories, and be willing to analyze what a child is trying to do. Remember that when we analyze and synthesize, we are practicing the same levels of thinking we expect of our students.

Must I carry the KOI with me at all times?

No, that's not realistic with your busy day. Instead, many teachers place their KOI folder with their plan book. Then, they see it every day and are reminded to tally any earlier observations. Consider placing Post-it™ Note pads around the room at strategic places. These enable you to make a quick note about a child to be tallied later. Tallying as consistently as you can enables you to remember most examples.

Does my effort really matter? Few of the students I nominate are identified gifted because their test results are not high enough to make the district cut off.

Your professional judgment is a crucial part of this process. We are eager to recognize a broader spectrum of students' talents and advanced potentials than objective tests alone can measure. Your insights could help others realize the need to balance subjective and objective information in order to identify multiple kinds of talents in all populations. Furthermore, your observations matter because whether or not a student is officially identified as gifted, you recognize the student's advanced responses and can immediately initiate the appropriate differentiation in your classroom. Your efforts enable you to respond to all learners, including those who are above average, high achievers, bright, or gifted.

Should I also write an anecdote to explain each tally?

That would benefit you, if you have the opportunity, but it is not required. Many times you are too busy to stop and write any comments. Some teachers have found that marking the tally on the KOI serves as a memory prompt that later enables you to recall and record the specific incident that resulted in the tally. Categorizing the observed behavior helps you to remember it.

Some behaviors fit in more than one category. Should I make multiple tallies for one behavior?

No, only tally once for each observed behavior. When a behavior fits several categories, tally in the category of your first or strongest impression. Because

Kingore, B. (2001). The Kingore Observation Inventory (KOI). 2nd ed. Austin, TX: Professional Associates Publishing.

so many clues are being considered, the pattern of the student's strengths will emerge over time.

I am worried if it is right to identify primary children. Aren't we just identifying children who come from enriched environments? Won't all children reach the same plateau by third grade?

Rather than puzzle over the quantity and quality of a child's previous experiences, the appropriate action is to respond to the needs and readiness level of each student. Olympic coaches work with primary children demonstrating advanced physical skills; they don't anticipate that all children will have the same physical talents by third grade. Music and art teachers encourage young fine art talents without assuming that all children will reach the same plateau. If a child is demonstrating advanced academic behaviors in one or more areas, we should provide the child with the most appropriate level of challenging content. If educators continue to respond to the demonstrated readiness level of each child, it is unlikely that all children will plateau at the same level of skills and achievements at third grade.

We do want to encourage parents and others to provide as many enriching experiences as possible for their child, but as educators, we accept all children where they are and help them advance learning as quickly as they are able. Children from enriched environments should receive that same opportunity.

Do most gifted students show up equally in all of the categories?

Very few people are globally gifted. The behaviors of most gifted students result in tallies in only three or four of the categories. Indeed, part of the instructional value of the KOI is to analyze the pattern of strengths for each child as revealed by the categories in which tallies are marked.

May I encourage students to think divergently ("Try to think of something no one else will think of."), or will this skew the results of the KOI?

Please, continually encourage all your students to think as complexly and divergently as possible. The KOI seeks behaviors that are characteristic of giftedness. Other students will not show these advanced behaviors as frequently and will score smaller numbers of tallies despite your encouragement. Remember to <u>encourage</u> high-levels of thinking, but do not <u>program</u> the response that you are trying to elicit.

How many tallies signify that a child is gifted?

There is no absolute number of tallies that determines giftedness. What is significant is the number of tallies and kinds of categories tallied for each student relative to the number of provided opportunities or in relation to the norms for

Kingore, B. (2001). <u>The Kingore Observation Inventory (KOI)</u>. 2nd ed. Austin, TX: Professional Associates Publishing.

your district (see Developing District Norms for the KOI on page 44 in this chapter). The number of tallies varies from population to population dependent upon the students' backgrounds and the range of opportunities provided in the classroom.

The number of tallies in itself is not as crucial a factor as the analysis of those tallies in regard to a student's needs and strengths. For example, when all the tallies are marked in one skill area, analysis may suggest continued enrichment instead of the need for total curriculum differentiation for that student. Or, if all the tallies are recorded in only the last week of observation, the analysis may suggest a student whose potential is just emerging. Guidelines for analyzing the results of a KOI observation period are shared earlier in this chapter on pages 36 through 40.

Is it possible to have too many tallies?

Yes. You are looking for a pattern of behaviors over a period of time. Dozens of tallies per student are not required and probably demand more time with record-keeping than you have to spare. Documenting behaviors with the KOI should not interfere in any substantial way with your regular classroom duties. It is meant to cause you to focus more concretely on gifted behaviors, encourage you to incorporate more learning experiences in your class that involve students in high-level thinking, and be a specific guide in identifying any gifted students in your class. Implementing the KOI system should not be a demanding, time-ladened job. It should blend naturally into the school day.

My state has many stipulations about what must be taught in various subject areas. How can I teach all that is required and still have time for activities that elicit gifted behaviors?

As you consider implementing a KOI activity, analyze which skill or content connections are possible with your curriculum. The KOI activities are intended as "instead of" rather than "more of". For example, a teacher might think, "Instead of that task I had students do the last time I taught this topic, I can integrate this open-ended KOI learning experience to teach this concept."

Chapter 5, Techniques, provides specific methods for incorporating the KOI process into most topics and subject areas. The techniques are designed to minimize teacher preparation time, maximize content connections, and elicit high-level thinking responses from students. In addition, many of the activities suggested in Chapter 6 readily apply to multiple content areas. Activities such as Alphabet Time, Word Web, Venn diagrams, Question That (a bulletin board), Draw Starts, and PMI are a few of the numerous activities designed to apply to multiple contents.

Many state standards and skills lend themselves directly to high-level thinking activities and open-ended learning experiences that form the core of the KOI process. For example, finding the main idea, categorizing by common

Kingore, B. (2001). <u>The Kingore Observation Inventory (KOI)</u>. 2nd ed. Austin, TX: Professional Associates Publishing.

attributes, predicting outcomes, determining cause and effect, problem solving, and finding patterns are all skills requiring the high-level thinking modeled in the KOI activities. Thus, the open-ended learning experiences suggested by the KOI process should be incorporated in your regular instructional day and help you teach many skills more effectively.

What does it mean if I don't have any tallies for my class in one or two of the categories?

It could indeed suggest that none of your students have strengths in that area. However, it also could suggest that more stimuli in those categories would benefit your children. In field testing, several teachers reported that when they had no tallies, or very few tallies in a category, they purposely incorporated more learning experiences for that category in their teaching. Then, they could be sure that they provided students ample opportunities to exhibit gifted behaviors in each category.

Should just the classroom teacher mark the KOI?

Any professional educator who interacts with or observes a student should be encouraged to tally observed gifted behaviors on the classroom KOI. For example, a resource teacher working with students may observe a behavior to tally; an administrator visiting the classroom might also tally an observed behavior. The goal is to record a pattern of the gifted behaviors students exhibit in each classroom. Educators should work together toward that goal. However, avoid duplicate tallying of the same behavior by more than one person.

How can I be sure if a student's behavior is high enough to earn a tally?

The guideline is to tally responses that exceed expectations for the grade level. Tally students whose behaviors bubble up beyond core curriculum responses. If you are uncertain about whether a behavior should be tallied, write a short note about the behavior and store it with your KOI folder. As you gain experience through observing students over substantial periods of time, your uncertainty may resolve itself. Furthermore, consider sharing your observation with another colleague, and talk together about possible interpretations. Both of you may enjoy and benefit from the professional conversation as you share insights about students and classroom observations. Another solid idea is to provide additional challenging opportunities for students in the category of the original behavior in question. Observe these additional opportunities to confirm if the student's responses are typical or more advanced.

Kingore, B. (2001). The Kingore Observation Inventory (KOI). 2nd ed. Austin, TX: Professional Associates Publishing.

CHAPTER 4
Parental Assessment

Perry alludes to the peril of being the parent of a gifted child: "The world is sympathetic to children who face learning and physical challenges and to their families but is not as eager to talk about the problems associated with being gifted (1998, 229).

Parents have unique opportunities to observe their children's advanced behaviors. For example, only a parent of one of these four children would know: that Don expressed himself so clearly in complete sentences at 18 months that others assumed him to be much older; that Sheri taught herself to use the computer at age four by watching her dad without him realizing; that, at age nine, Anna built complex cities of Legos™ and asked about the problems of urban decay; or that Craig independently studied hieroglyphics and Greek to extend his interest in archeology at age twelve.

Unfortunately, parent nominations are not universally used as a criterion in gifted identification. Many educators assume that all parents consider their children to be gifted. Yet, parents occasionally startle educators by being unrealistically stringent in their analysis of superior abilities. As one parent noted regarding advanced language, "Most of the children I know read before kindergarten. It seems rather typical."

Parents are not trained in gifted education, and they have a specialized perspective. Thus, some parents underestimate children's abilities, and others overestimate them, as when parents' egos supersede their child's needs. However, many research studies conclude that parents are basically good identifiers and that their input is especially important to ensure identification of special populations (Ciha, T.E., 1974; Greenlaw, J. & McIntosh, M., 1988; Jacobs, J. D., 1971; Slocumb, P. D. & Payne, R. K., 2000). Informal data from parents should be part of an ongoing assessment used to complement rather than confirm test scores or other data (Colangelo & Davis, 1997). Roedell warned that with the instability of children's tests scores, "It would hardly be reasonable to use prediction of concurrent test performance as the sole standard for evaluating the usefulness of parent information" (1980, 61).

Kingore, B. (2001). The Kingore Observation Inventory (KOI). 2nd ed. Austin, TX: Professional Associates Publishing.

Checklists are a typical format for eliciting parent information. One limitation of listing behaviors on checklists is that it overlooks the possibility that some gifted children may be most remarkable not for what they do, but for how they do it. A second problem is, to be a reasonable length, the checklist cannot be comprehensive enough to include all the behaviors by which a child might display gifted potential. These limitations are overcome with an open-ended format that collects parents' anecdotal comments regarding their observations and insights of their child.

Rather than quantitatively mark a checklist, the Parent Information Form (PIF) enables parents to supply specific examples of the behaviors and traits they have observed about their gifted child at home and in other family situations. The PIF is based upon the seven categories of gifted behaviors on the KOI. The items listed in each category are restated to include parent-observable behaviors. Then, each category provides space for parents to write examples of things their child said or did that relate to that category.

Limitations of the PIF	Recommendations
The anecdotes require time to read, interpret, and score.	This limitation is also an asset inasmuch as the time educators invest in learning about the home environment aids in understanding the whole child.
Parents may not read and write fluently in English.	All parent forms must be translated into the home language if it is other than English.
Some parents are reluctant to complete paperwork for formal agencies-- "How will this information be used?"	Recommend interviews or home visits with parents who might feel uncomfortable responding to the information form.
Some parents feel less able to complete the PIF. It could seem to be a test of a parent's ability or writing skills.	Provide assistance and support by having another adult scribe for the parent. Or, in a teacher-parent conference, use the PIF to focus discussions about the child. Scribe the responses, or allow the parent to take the PIF to complete and return later.
Some educators are concerned about the parent's accuracy.	Encourage parents to substantiate their anecdotes with product examples.

Encourage parents to support their anecdotes on the PIF with a small set of the child's products that illustrate each observed gifted characteristic. An article is included in this chapter to guide parents' development of a six to ten item portfolio advocating their child's exceptional learning needs. The first page of the article is intended for educators as an overview of the process. The next two pages of the article outline for parents the objectives, procedure, and examples of products that might be informative.

Kingore, B. (2001). The Kingore Observation Inventory (KOI). 2nd ed. Austin: Professional Associates Publishing.

Parent Information Form
Grades K through 3
Derived from The Kingore Observation Inventory (KOI)

STUDENT _____ GRADE _____

PARENT _____ DATE _____

TEACHER _____ SCHOOL _____

Parents have unique opportunities to see their children at play, at work, and in family settings. Please, share your observations with us. This form and the similar KOI completed by the teacher will be included with other data to increase our understanding of your child's needs.

ADVANCED LANGUAGE

Uses words that seem advanced for the age-level expectations
Rewords own language for younger or less mature children
Explains how unrelated things are similar
Uses words for time concepts (clock and calendar) accurately
Uses similes, metaphors, or analogies; "A ___ is really like a ___ because ___"
Asks questions about words (in print or oral language)

Examples from above of things my child said: _____

_____

_____

ANALYTICAL THINKING

Demonstrates complex or abstract thinking
Analyzes household or school tasks
Notices a surprising depth of details about surroundings
Takes apart and reassembles things or ideas with skill
Expresses relationships between past and present experiences
Makes up songs, stories, or riddles about experiences
Organizes collections of things uniquely; likes to plan or arrange things

Examples from above of things my child said or did: _____

_____

_____

Kingore, B. (2001). The Kingore Observation Inventory (KOI). 2nd ed. Austin: Professional Associates Publishing.

Parent Information Form: Grades K through 3   **Page 2**

MEANING MOTIVATION
Is philosophical Asks surprisingly intellectual questions Is curious; experiments Demonstrates an unexpected depth of knowledge in one or more areas Exhibits intense task commitment and energy when pursuing interests Remembers! Is independent

Examples from above of things my child said or did: _____

_____

_____

_____

PERSPECTIVE
Explains another's point of view Shows dimension, angle, or perspective in art, writing, math solutions, or problem solving Creates complex shapes, patterns, or graphics Applies left and right without prompting Adds interesting details to enhance products

Examples from above of things my child said or did: _____

_____

_____

_____

SENSE OF HUMOR
Says or does something indicating an unexpected, sophisticated humor Catches an adult's subtle humor Understands and uses puns and riddles "Plays" with language Develops humorous ideas to an extreme

Examples from above of things my child said or did: _____

_____

_____

_____

Kingore, B. (2001). The Kingore Observation Inventory (KOI). 2nd ed. Austin: Professional Associates Publishing.

Parent Information Form: Grades K through 3   **Page 3**

SENSITIVITY
Cares deeply; intense concern for human issues Tries to take action to help someone in need Expresses feelings through words or art Explains others' feelings Displays a strong sense of fairness Expresses high expectations of self and others Seems to overreact at times

Examples from above of things my child said or did: _____

_____

_____

_____

ACCELERATED LEARNING
Learns new things quickly with minimum practice Uses multiple characteristics when discussing items Reads passages at an advanced, fluent reading level for the age-level expectations Explains the meaning of what has been read Demonstrates an unexpected mastery of math or science concepts Uses a dictionary, encyclopedia, map, atlas, or computer to gain advanced information Creates products which seem advanced for the age-level expectations

Examples from above of things my child said or did: _____

_____

_____

_____

Other information I would like you to know about my child: _____

_____

_____

_____

_____

_____

Please return this form to your child's teacher by: _____

Kingore, B. (2001). The Kingore Observation Inventory (KOI). 2nd ed. Austin: Professional Associates Publishing.

Parent Information Form
Grades 4 through 8
Derived from The Kingore Observation Inventory (KOI)

STUDENT _____ GRADE _____

PARENT _____ DATE _____

TEACHER _____ SCHOOL _____

Parents have unique opportunities to see their children at play, at work, and in family settings. Please, share your observations with us. This form and the similar KOI completed by the teacher will be included with other data to increase our understanding of your child's needs.

ADVANCED LANGUAGE

Uses a large vocabulary and more precise language than expected for the age-level
Is unusually descriptive in conversations or writings
Expresses similes, metaphors, or analogies; "A _____ is really like
  a _____ because _____."
Modifies language for less experienced listeners
Ably explains complex concepts to others
Uses verbal skills to handle conflicts or influence others

Examples from above of things my child said: _____

_____

_____

ANALYTICAL THINKING

Able to abstract and generalize information
Notices a surprising depth of details about surroundings
Thinks logically; presents arguments logically
Thinks critically; may lead to skepticism
Recognizes relationships or patterns between ideas or experiences
Enjoys analyzing and solving difficult problems
Enjoys planning and organizing

Examples from above of things my child said or did: _____

_____

_____

Kingore, B. (2001). The Kingore Observation Inventory (KOI). 2nd ed. Austin: Professional Associates Publishing.

Parent Information Form: Grades 4 through 8

MEANING MOTIVATION

Is philosophical
Has a questioning attitude; asks intellectual questions about complex topics
Generates multiple new ideas and solutions to problems; ingenious
Demonstrates in-depth information in areas beyond age-expectations
Remembers! (may retell an experience, story, or video almost verbatim)
Displays high levels of task commitment and energy when pursuing interests
Eager to do things differently; independent

Examples from above of things my child said or did: _____

_____

_____

PERSPECTIVE

Explains another's point of view
Approaches problems from an unusual perspective in oral discussions, art, writing, and
       math solutions, or problem solving
Expresses past, present, and future aspects of an issue
Develops advanced or unique graphic products and patterns
Appreciates the beauty and value of things

Examples from above of things my child said or did: _____

_____

_____

SENSE OF HUMOR

Says or does something indicating a sense of humor beyond the age-level expectations
Uses humor to gain approval of others
Catches an adult's subtle humor
Uses figurative language and puns for humorous effect
Uses humor that may be absurd or far-out

Examples from above of things my child said or did: _____

_____

_____

Kingore, B. (2001). The Kingore Observation Inventory (KOI). 2nd ed. Austin: Professional Associates Publishing.

Parent Information Form: Grades 4 through 8   **Page 3**

SENSITIVITY
Exhibits intense concern for human issues
Intuitive and insightful of others' needs and feelings
Expresses feelings through words or art
Cares deeply but may mask sensitivity
Bases friendships on similarity of interest rather than age
Displays a strong sense of justice; demands fairness and consistency
Demonstrates high expectations of self and others
Prefers to be a loner part of the time
Overreacts at times

Examples from above of things my child said or did: _____

_____

_____

ACCELERATED LEARNING
Demonstrates knowledge beyond the age-level expectations
Comprehends and uses symbols with an unexpected ability
Reads fluently, more like an adult; comprehends with advanced understanding
Understands and uses advanced ideas, concepts, or implications
Learns easily and with a minimum of practice
Creates products that are advanced for the age-level expectations
Accesses data with ease using an unexpected variety of tools

Examples from above of things my child said or did: _____

_____

_____

Other information I would like you to know about my child: _____

_____

_____

_____

_____

Please return this form to your child's teacher by: _____

Kingore, B. (2001). <u>The Kingore Observation Inventory (KOI)</u>. 2nd ed. Austin: Professional Associates Publishing.

Holistic Scoring
of the Parent Information Form

Scoring of the Parent Information Form (PIF) parallels the Holistic Scoring of the KOI observations. Using this evaluation strategy, the scorer considers all of the anecdotes and information shared by a parent and aggregates the data into a holistic judgment. The objective is to interpret behaviors typical of gifted learners from the family's perceptions of the child's strengths and needs.

Avoid using the rubric to assign numerical values to each category and then totaling the results. This process implies that students exhibiting behaviors in many categories are more advanced than students who consistently exhibit advanced behaviors in a few categories. This implication is not always valid. A student's giftedness may be remarkable for the clearly outstanding examples that the parent describes in only a few categories.

SCORING PROCEDURE

- If desired, place Post-it™ Notes over the names and data on each PIF to ensure anonymity.
- Initially, skim all of the PIFs as an overview to determine the most typical responses.
- Use the holistic rubric to score each PIF.
- Interrater reliability is established through one of the two following practices.
  1. A single reviewer evaluates all PIFs.
  2. Two or three reviewers score PIFs separately and compare analyses for consistency. The first reviewer reads a PIF, scores it according to the rubric, and records the score on the back of the form. The second reviewer reads the same PIF, scores it, and records the score on the back. If the assessments match, the score is recorded. If there is disagreement, a third reviewer evaluates.
- On some PIFs, discussion ensues between reviewers to clarify and establish a consensus.
- The PIF score is recorded on a Student Profile form if the PIF is used as one criterion in the assessment of gifted potential.

RUBRIC			
1 **Average**	**2** **Above Average**	**3** **Superior**	**4** **Very Superior**
Anecdotes suggest behaviors typical of the age-level expectations	Anecdotes imply occasional sparks of potential beyond the age-level Responses are characteristic of high-achieving students	Anecdotes describe behaviors that consistently exceed the age-level expectations Responses are more complex	Anecdotes signal clearly outstanding behaviors; remarkable for age Responses substantially exceed expectations
Recommendation: Continued enrichment of the environment	**Recommendation:** Continued observation and challenge	**Recommendation:** Further assessment of gifted potential	**Recommendation:** Gifted identification with no reservations

Kingore, B. (2001). <u>The Kingore Observation Inventory (KOI)</u>. 2nd ed. Austin: Professional Associates Publishing.

Parental Assessment of Giftedness:
Developing Portfolios to Document Gifted Learners' Talents

by Bertie Kingore

One ignored role of portfolios is parental assessment of children's exceptional learning needs. The products children develop provide clear documentation of achievements and potential.

INTRODUCTION FOR EDUCATORS

Parents have the right and need to be active partners with schools in planning and supporting the education of their children. When identifying gifted potential, districts benefit from parental assessment information in forms other than checklists. Portfolios enable parents to be proactive instead of reactive. They encourage parents to be viable members in the assessment process by preparing concrete examples of children's abilities and needs.

Portfolios will increase the credibility of parental assessment of gifted potential by documenting the depth and complexity of the child's work. Documentation through products illustrates each gifted characteristic of the child that the parent has observed, and it increases the likelihood that the parent's perception of the child's needs is respected. However, if parents overestimate the advanced potential of a child, school personnel can meet with the parent to share a small set of typical examples of grade-level products to compare with the parent's selections and concretely substantiate that the child's learning needs are best met through the core curriculum rather than advanced contents.

Parental development of a portfolio to substantiate a student's gifted potential is particularly needed when the child is:
- Part of an educational system that values parental assessment in identifying and serving advanced learners and wants to increase the validity of that assessment;
- Very young and not yet recognized as advanced by adults at school;
- A member of a diverse culture whose gifted behaviors are more difficult to assess in a mainstream classroom;

- Advanced in one subject area but not all;
- New to the area so the child's potential has not been demonstrated in that school; or
- A student in a school where the curriculum in all classes is not differentiated for able learners.

GUIDING PARENTS' SELECTION OF PRODUCTS

Parents need guidance in selecting products that are appropriate and effective. Share your district's mission statement and definition of giftedness with parents so they can more directly match selections in the portfolio to the school's philosophical stance. For example, when your school's program serves academic giftedness in language arts, math, social studies, and science, you want parents to include products that demonstrate advanced talents in one or more of those areas.

The product list included in the parent section is meant to prompt ideas of a wide range of products from home that might be appropriate for students' portfolios (adapted from Kingore, 1999a). A variation of these products specifically suited to very young children is shared in Communicator (Kingore, 1999b).

The following factors increase the assessment value of a portfolio.
- A portfolio should be an integral reflection of what a child has learned rather than artificial activities and isolated skills.
- Products that effectively advocate giftedness demonstrate depth, complexity, and the ability to process and reorganize information to produce a product unique for that age or level.
- The products should help substantiate that the child's interest and expertise in topics are not typical.
- Products selected for a portfolio must be completed by the child without assistance.

If applicable, copy the parent section of this article for parents to facilitate their assessment and development of a portfolio. Specify with whom the parents should share the portfolio once the product selection process is complete.

REFERENCE
Kingore, B. (1999a). Assessment: Time-Saving Procedures for Busy Teachers, 2nd ed. Austin: Professional Associates Publishing.

Kingore, B. (1999b). Portfolios: Documenting the needs of young gifted learners. Communicator: California Association for the Gifted, 30(4), 10-11, 46-47.

Reprinted from: Kingore, B. Texas Association for the Gifted and Talented. Tempo. Spring, 2000.
Kingore, B. (2001). The Kingore Observation Inventory (KOI). 2nd ed. Austin: Professional Associates Publishing.

Parental Assessment:

Developing a Portfolio to Document Your Child's Talents

by Bertie Kingore

Prepare a small selection of your child's products to document learning achievements and advanced potential.

Schools want to provide opportunities for children to learn as much as they are ready and able. Your insight about your child's at-home demonstrations of learning heighten our understanding of your child's needs. A portfolio increases the credibility of how you advocate for your child by documenting the depth and complexity of your child's work. Product examples increase the likelihood that your perception of your child's needs is accepted and respected by educators inasmuch as the products illustrate each gifted characteristic you have observed.

HOW DO PARENTS BEGIN?

- Use a pocket folder or photo album (one-inch thickness) as a portfolio container to organize a few products your child has produced. Photographs can be used to represent large or three-dimensional items.
- Keep the portfolio small. Six to ten items are probably sufficient to represent your child's talents. A small sampling of carefully selected products makes a more thoughtful presentation than a large scrapbook approach. Educators have demanding work loads, and they are more likely to have time to attend with interest to a sampling.
- Date each product. It is important for authenticity and achievement-level comparisons to note when each item was completed.
- If needed for clarity, prepare brief explanations of how your child demonstrated a specific characteristic through that product or during the process of completing that product.
- Briefly describe additional, exceptional behaviors that your child frequently displays, such as independent thinking, problem solving, and asking questions about topics or concepts not typically addressed by children. You are in a unique posi-

tion to recount to others the processes as well as the products of your child's learning.
- Share some written examples of your child's expressed perceptions of school that suggest advanced sensitivity and unexpected points of view. Use your child's own words to describe the challenge or lack of it in learning situations. For example, children often tell adults that they are bored. What does your child really mean if she or he says "bored"? Record what your child says about when and how they are bored at school.

GUIDELINES FOR SELECTING PORTFOLIO PRODUCTS

The included portfolio products list is meant to prompt ideas of a wide range of products that might be appropriate in your child's portfolio. Select products that are an integral reflection of what your child has learned rather than artificial activities and isolated skills. Let the portfolio represent the main idea you want educators to understand about your child.

Products that document giftedness demonstrate depth, complexity, and the ability to process and reorganize information to produce a product unique for that age or grade level. The products may substantiate your child's interest and expertise in topics that are not typical.

Products selected for a portfolio must be completed by the child without assistance for two important reasons. Foremost, because your child's self-esteem is influenced by his or her competent, personal achievements. (Remaking products into adult projects risks the children acquiring feelings of doubt and ambiguity about their abilities.) Secondly, the portfolio is taken more seriously when the products look child-appropriate rather than adult-level perfect. (Educators may be suspicious of products that suggest extensive adult intervention.)

A FINAL ENCOURAGEMENT

Be an advocate rather than an adversary. You want what all parents want for their children: the opportunity for children to learn as much as they are ready and able to learn. All children deserve to learn at their optimum readiness level--even the gifted. Be an advocate whose only motive is to ensure your child's right to an appropriate education. If we are motivated by children's best interests and not our own ego needs, our efforts will usually guide us in the most appropriate direction.

Reprinted from: Kingore, B. Texas Association for the Gifted and Talented. Tempo. Spring, 2000.
Kingore, B. (2001). The Kingore Observation Inventory (KOI). 2nd ed. Austin: Professional Associates Publishing.

Examples of Portfolio Products

PRODUCT	EXPLANATION	PURPOSE
Art	Art pieces should include the child's natural, creative explorations and interpretations (rather than crafts).	Art reflects developmental levels, interests, graphic talents, abstract thinking, and creativity.
Audio tapes	Tape the child's explanation of advanced concepts, philosophical viewpoints, musical creations, problem solutions, and ideas.	Audio tapes verify vocabulary, fluency, creativity, high-order thinking, and concept depth.
Computer	Document computer skills through applications of more sophisticated software and programs created by the child.	Computer-generated products indicate computer literacy, analysis, content-related academic skills, and applied concepts.
Dictations	Write your child's dictated explanation of a product or process. Prompt these dictations with statements such as: "Tell me how you did that."	Dictations increase adults' understanding of the why and how of what children do. It may indicate advanced vocabulary, high-level thinking, fluency, and content depth.
Graphs or charts	Some children produce graphs or charts to represent relationships, formulate problems, illustrate math solutions, and demonstrate the results of independent investigations.	Graphs or charts demonstrate specific skills or concepts applied in the task, high-level thinking, data recording strategies, and organizational skills.
Photographs	Photograph your child's math patterns, creative projects, dioramas, sculptures, constructions, experiments, models, or organizational systems.	Photographs represent three-dimensional products. They provide a record when no paper product is feasible.
Reading level	Provide one or two examples of books or printed material your child reads independently (not material your child has memorized). Include your child's reflection of the book to demonstrate analysis skills.	All children do not read and interpret advanced-level materials. However, since advanced learning opportunities often require reading independence, educators are interested in students' reading levels.
Research	Gifted students usually have information and expertise beyond the age-level expectations in one or more areas. Share examples of the independent studies pursued by your child.	Research products reveal specific interests, synthesis, content depth, and complexity of learners.
Video tape	Video tapes are wonderful ways to document performing arts and your child's learning process. They are less applicable to substantiate academic skill development due to the equipment and time necessary to show the tape. Limit tape entries to three or four minutes if they are to be reviewed by educators.	A video presents a significant visual record and integration of skills and behaviors. When recording group interactions, a video can demonstrate interpersonal and leadership skills.
Written products	Provide examples of original works written by the child including stories, reports, scientific observations, poems, or reflections.	Written products may demonstrate advanced language, thinking, organization, meaning construction, concept depth, and complexity.

Reprinted from: Kingore, B. Texas Association for the Gifted and Talented. Tempo. Spring, 2000.
Kingore, B. (2001). The Kingore Observation Inventory (KOI). 2nd ed. Austin: Professional Associates Publishing.

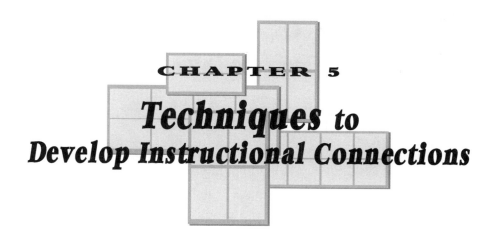

CHAPTER 5
Techniques to
Develop Instructional Connections

Teachers do not need extra content to teach or more instructional things to prepare! In that manner, teachers are very like advanced learners--they do not need more to do, they need a different way to succeed. The KOI system is not based on extra activities teachers must find time to do. The process works effectively and efficiently when teachers incorporate simple techniques to prompt KOI behaviors in their regular curriculum. The techniques are designed to minimize teachers' preparation time, maximize content connections to the KOI categories, and encourage high-level thinking responses from students.

The KOI Open-ended Questions and Statements that Increase Thinking is one technique teachers find useful. The KOI questions and statements, organized according to the seven categories of the KOI, are designed to elicit advanced responses from students. As the completed examples of this process illustrate, these open-ended prompts apply across grade levels to multiple, varied topics such as dinosaurs, weather, the Civil War, and ecology. Use these ideas to generate high-level thinking opportunities more consistently throughout your curriculum.

SCAMPER to Generate Productive Thinking is another technique for developing instructional connections. Developed by Alex Osborn and Bob Eberle, it is a brainstorming device that teachers and students successfully use to generate new ideas. Personalize SCAMPER to your instruction by using the technique to guide brainstorming connections to your areas of study. Record your generated ideas on the SCAMPER form at the end of this chapter. Then, correlate those ideas to the KOI categories as the completed examples in this chapter illustrate. SCAMPER applications are provided for <u>The Very Hungry Caterpillar</u>, and the topics of the balance of power in the government and coins and dollars.

Use both techniques as checklists to generate new ideas related to your curriculum. As you plan a topic of study, allow five to ten minutes to skim the prompts on either technique and record any instructional connections you produce. Frequently, you think of connections beyond the prompts as the process inspires your creative ideas. The depth and breadth of your results can be amazing!

Kingore, B. (2001). <u>The Kingore Observation Inventory (KOI)</u>. 2nd ed. Austin: Professional Associates Publishing.

— KOI Open-ended Questions and Statements —
that Increase Thinking

To increase the level of students' responses, use these ideas to generate high-level thinking opportunities related to each of your units or topics. Specifically, as you plan your unit, allow five to ten minutes to skim these prompts. Mark any for which you think of a useful connection to your topics or concepts. The examples that follow for dinosaurs, weather, the Civil War, and ecology model the results of that brainstorming process.

Advanced Language

- What are other words you could use instead of _____?
- This _____ is like _____.
- How many different meanings can you think of for _____?
- Explain _____ to someone who does not understand.
- What could you say to _____ when there is a problem?
- Describe the appearance of _____?
- Explain which five words you think are the most significant to this topic or concept.

Analytical Thinking

- What might happen if _____?
- Name all the attributes you can think of for _____.
- Get ideas from _____ to improve _____.
- How is _____ different from _____? How are they similar?
- What could be done to make _____ more effective?
- How could we organize _____?
- What makes this unique?
- Look at this _____. Tell me all the things we would need to make one like it.
- Illustrate or explain one pattern you have identified related to this topic.

Meaning Motivation

- The answer is _____. Think of as many questions as you can that have that answer.
- List all the facts you can think of about _____.
- What/why/how is _____?
- Why does _____ happen when _____?
- What might happen if _____?
- What philosophical issues are involved?
- What are the unanswered questions related to this topic?

Kingore, B. (2001). The Kingore Observation Inventory (KOI). 2nd ed. Austin: Professional Associates Publishing.

Perspective

- If you were _____, what would you see/hear/taste/feel/smell?
- How would _____ be thought of by _____?
- What would _____ look like if you were _(different places/positions/sizes)_?
- How would _____ affect a _____?
- What might _____ think about that?
- Explain, to someone who has never been to _____, how to get there.
- How might a person living 150 years ago respond?
- Explain the opposing viewpoint of this issue.

Sense of Humor

- What might happen if _____ had _(some humorous attribute)_ instead of _____?
- The funniest thing about _____ is _____.
- If you put _____ and _____ together, you could call it _(a new word)_ and it could _____.
- Instead of _____, it would be funnier if _____.
- Explain what "you drive me up the wall" means. (Substitute other appropriate examples of figurative language.)
- Draw a cartoon strip that incorporates information about this topic.

Sensitivity

- If you were a _(topic related item)_, you'd be _____ because _____.
- How would _____ feel if _____?
- What do you feel about _____?
- How does _____ apply to others?
- The fair thing to do is/was _____.
- What do you think is the best thing to do to help _____?
- What are the ethical ramifications?

Accelerated Learning

- What symbols could be used to represent _____?
- What sources might have the greatest depth and complexity of information about _____?
- How many things can you think of that have _____ and _____? (two attributes)
- List all the things you can think of that are _____, _____, and _____. (three attributes)
- Make up a code to _____.
- Relate these factors to past, present, and future trends.

Kingore, B. (2001). The Kingore Observation Inventory (KOI). 2nd ed. Austin: Professional Associates Publishing.

Dinosaurs

Advanced Language
- What are all the words you could use instead of large?
- Explain what a fossil is to someone who does not understand.
- Describe the appearance of a Tyrannosaurus.

Analytical Thinking
- Name all the attributes you can think of for a carnivore.
- How is an Apatosaurus different from a construction crane? How are they similar?
- What makes a Velociraptor unique?

Meaning Motivation
- The answer is: extinct. Think of as many questions as you can which have that answer.
- What might happen if dinosaurs still lived in some parts of our country?
- Why do scientists not know the actual color of dinosaurs?
- What enabled dinosaurs to develop so large?

Perspective
- If you were a dinosaur, what would you see/hear/taste/feel/smell?
- What would our school look like to a Pterodactylus?
- What might an elephant think about a dinosaur if one were still alive?

Sense of Humor
- What funny things might happen if a Stegosaurus had wings instead of plates along its back?
- If you combined Pterodactylus and a Tyrannosaurus, what would you call it? What would be funny about what it could do?

Sensitivity
- If you were a dinosaur, which one would you want to be? Why?
- If two people found a dinosaur fossil at the same time and they both wanted to keep it, what would be the fair thing to do?

Accelerated Learning
- Make up a symbol for each attribute or kind of dinosaur.
- Other than these books in our room, what sources might we use to find out more about dinosaurs?
- How many different things can you think of that are very big and of great interest to scientists?

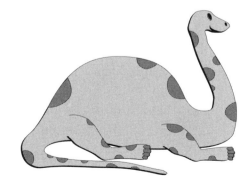

Kingore, B. (2001). The Kingore Observation Inventory (KOI). 2nd ed. Austin: Professional Associates Publishing.

Weather

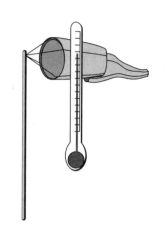

Advanced Language
- What other words could you use instead of wind?
- This thermometer is like _____.
- How many ways can you describe rain?
- Explain what a cloud is to someone who does not understand.

Analytical Thinking
- What might happen if it never rained?
- Name all the attributes you can think of for lightning.
- Incorporate ideas from cooking to demonstrate a weather phenomenon.
- How is snow different from rain? How are they similar?
- What could be done to make storm warnings more effective?
- What makes a tornado spin counter clockwise North of the equator?
- Look at this wind gauge, and tell me all the things we would need to make one like it.
- Explain an example of the use of patterns in weather forecasting.

Meaning Motivation
- The answer is: precipitation. Think of as many questions as you can with that answer.
- List all the facts you can think of about fog.
- What is the value of the wind chill factor? Is it more or less important than temperature?
- When might a rainbow appear on a clear day?
- What might happen if sleet were hot?

Perspective
- If you were in a cloud, what would you see/hear/taste/feel/smell?
- How would today's weather forecasting instruments be viewed by the Lewis and Clark expedition?
- What would rain look like if you were underwater?
- What would fog mean to a pilot?
- Role play the different ways farmers might react to a variety of weather conditions.

Sense of Humor
- What might happen if wind blew up and down?
- The funniest thing about thunder is _____.
- If you put snow and fog together, you could call it snog and it could _____.
- Instead of clouds, it would be funnier if _____.
- Explain what "raining cats and dogs" means. Create and illustrate additional figurative language examples involving weather.

Sensitivity
- If you were a type of precipitation, you'd be a _____ because _____.
- How might a river feel if it flooded?
- Are there any positive results of damaging weather? Explain.
- How does wind chill apply to people?
- What do you think is the best thing to do to help victims of weather-related disasters?
- What are the ethical ramifications of individuals hoarding supplies in advance of a weather disaster?

Accelerated Learning
- What symbols could be used to clarify weather maps?
- How many things can you think of that have both heat and light?
- List all the things you can think of that have moisture, wind, and clouds.
- Make up a code to warn of dangerous weather.

Kingore, B. (2001). The Kingore Observation Inventory (KOI). 2nd ed. Austin: Professional Associates Publishing.

The Civil War

Advanced Language
- What other words can be used instead of "secede"?
- Explain "state's rights" to someone who does not understand.
- How many different meanings can you think of for "union"?
- Which three-syllable words best describe the slavery issue?
- Explain which five words you think are the most significant to the Civil War.

Analytical Thinking
- What might have happened if the South had won the war?
- Name three attributes for "free state."
- How is a civil war different from a cross town football rivalry? How are they similar?
- How is a slave different from and similar to a machine?
- What could have been done to make plantations successful without using slaves?
- Explain one pattern you have identified related to the Civil War.
- Compare the underground railroad with a regular railroad.

Meaning Motivation
- The answer is: Confederacy. List as many questions as you can.
- What philosophical issues were involved after the Civil War?
- What is freedom to you? What is slavery to you?
- List all the facts you know about the causes of the Civil War.
- What are some unanswered questions about this period in history?
- Debate the issue of flying the Confederate flag over governmental buildings today.

Perspective
- If you were a slave in the South, what would you see/hear/smell/taste/feel?
- How might the Civil War be viewed by a soldier's wife/soldier/gun maker/slave?
- What would freedom mean if you were a plantation owner?
- What would a battlefield look like if you were a soldier's boot?
- Role play a conversation between a Northern and Southern land owner.
- Identify the priorities of Georgians during the Civil War, present times, and 100 years in the future.

Sense of Humor
- What might have happened if the soldiers had to fight with food instead of weapons?
- If you put an abolitionist and a circus performer together, you could _____.
- Explain how the expression "too many cooks can spoil the stew" relates to the Civil War.
- Draw cartoons illustrating key words from this historical period, such as: carpetbagger.

Sensitivity
- If you lived during the Civil War, what would be your role? Why?
- How would children feel if their fathers went to war?
- How would children feel if their parents were sold as slaves?
- How does "loyalty to one's own country" apply to the South during the war?
- The fair thing to do about state's rights would have been _____.

Accelerated Learning
- What symbols could be used for freedom?
- What can you think of that has both freedom and restriction?
- What things can you think of that are separate and part of a union?
- What sources might be used to find more in-depth information about freemen's lives after the war?

Kingore, B. (2001). <u>The Kingore Observation Inventory (KOI)</u>. 2nd ed. Austin: Professional Associates Publishing.

Ecology

Advanced Language
- What are other words you could use instead of "recycle"?
- This litter is like _____?
- How many different meanings can you think of for paper?
- Explain which five words you think are most significant to ecology.
- Explain what pollution is to someone who does not understand.

Analytical Thinking
- Name all the attributes you can think of for hazardous waste.
- Integrate ideas from alternate energy sources to purify emissions.
- How is "reduce" different from "reuse"? How are they similar?
- What could be done to make recycling more effective?
- What could we do to make an ecology club for our school unique?
- How could we organize a carpool for our neighborhood?

Meaning Motivation
- The answer is: trash. Think of as many questions as you can with that answer.
- List all the facts you can think of about air pollution. Rank them from most to least harmful.
- Why does water pollution occur? What are the most relevant issues affecting water pollution?
- What is the ethical thing to do if there is a chemical spill near a creek, river, or lake?
- What are the unanswered questions related to ecology?

Perspective
- If you were litter, what would you see/hear/taste/feel/smell?
- How might a Native American living 150 years ago respond to today's pollution problems?
- Respond to the concept of a hole in the ozone layer from the perspective of a senior citizen/factory owner/scientist..
- What would an oil spill mean to sea life?
- Role play what birds might think about exhaust emissions.

Sense of Humor
- What might happen if garbage cans burped?
- The funniest thing about the environment is _____.
- If you put a carpool and a bike together, you could call it _____, and it could _____.
- Instead of litter falling on the ground, it would be funnier if every time a person littered it _____.
- Explain what "down in the dumps" means.

Sensitivity
- If you were a paper product, you'd be a _____ because _____.
- How do you feel about flowers, gardens, and forests?
- How does recycling apply to others?
- What do you think is the best way to help animals whose habitat has been destroyed?
- What is the most appropriate thing to do when you see someone littering?

Accelerated Learning
- What symbols could be used for the terms reduce, reuse, and recycle?
- What sources might be used to find out more about local recycling issues?
- How many things can you think of that have beauty and are free?
- List all the things you can think of that are plastic and reusable.
- Make up a code to identify forms of pollution.
- Relate ecology issues to past, present, and future trends.

Kingore, B. (2001). <u>The Kingore Observation Inventory (KOI)</u>. 2nd ed. Austin: Professional Associates Publishing.

SCAMPER
to Generate Productive Thinking

SCAMPER is an acronym developed by Alex Osborn and Bob Eberle to expedite the brainstorming of new ideas and promote looking at old thoughts in new ways. When teachers become dissatisfied with the way they have taught something, they can use SCAMPER as a mental checklist to generate different ideas. Use the form of page 76 to record the results of your brainstorming.

 **ubstitute**
- who or what else
- instead
- another time
- another place

C ombine
- purposes
- ideas
- blend

A dapt
- what is like this
- what other ideas does this suggest

 odify
- change meaning, color, motion, sound, taste, shape, form

 **-inify**
- what to subtract
- smaller
- lighter
- slower

 **-agnify**
- what to add
- greater frequency
- larger and stronger
- multiply

 **ut to other uses**
- new ways to use
- other uses if modified

 liminate
- remove
- get rid of a quality
- get rid of a part

 earrange
- another layout
- another sequence
- pace

-everse
- opposites
- turn it backwards
- turn it upside down
- turn it inside out

Kingore, B. (2001). The Kingore Observation Inventory (KOI). 2nd ed. Austin: Professional Associates Publishing.

Avoid thinking of SCAMPER as a rigid sequence. It does not have to be completed in any certain order, and it is not necessary to develop ideas for all letters of the acronym each time. Personalize SCAMPER to your instruction by using the technique as an effective device to guide brainstorming about a skill or topic you want to teach. As an example, when teaching primary students about coins and dollars, SCAMPER to generate new possibilities, such as the examples that follow.

TOPIC: Coins and dollars

		KOI Categories				
Advanced Language	Analytical Thinking	Meaning Motivation	Perspective	Sense of Humor	Sensitivity	Accelerated Learning

S substitute:
(Provide self-locking plastic bags of Fruit Loops™, and ask students: "If one Fruit Loop equals one penny, show me with the Fruit Loops in your bag how many I need to make a dime.") Explain how you like or dislike using Fruit Loops™ instead of pennies.

Categories: Advanced Language, Analytical Thinking, Meaning Motivation

C combine:
(Provide paper replicas of coins, a hole punch, and some yarn.) Make coin necklaces by punching holes through a small number of the coins, stringing them, and determining how much their necklace is worth by counting and totaling the coin values.

Categories: Analytical Thinking, Accelerated Learning

A adapt:
Make up three questions to ask someone about how coins are made.

Categories: Advanced Language, Meaning Motivation

M modify:
Explain the benefits and problems if all coins were the same size.

Categories: Advanced Language, Analytical Thinking, Meaning Motivation

minify:
Explain what problems might result if we had no dollars or quarters and the only forms of money were pennies, nickels, and dimes? How might store owners feel about only having small coins?

Categories: Advanced Language, Analytical Thinking, Meaning Motivation, Sense of Humor, Sensitivity

magnify:
Explain how buying things in a store would be different if we had no coins and all we could use were dollar bills for our money? What if all we could use were dollar coins?

Categories: Advanced Language, Analytical Thinking, Meaning Motivation

P put to other use:
Try to figure out which coin is in a "feely box" without looking. Tell why you think it is that coin. What attributes can you determine by feeling? What can you not determine?

Categories: Advanced Language, Analytical Thinking, Meaning Motivation

R rearrange:
Put a penny, nickel, dime, quarter, and dollar coin in order by the size circle of each. What do you notice?

Categories: Advanced Language, Analytical Thinking

Kingore, B. (2001). The Kingore Observation Inventory (KOI). 2nd ed. Austin: Professional Associates Publishing.

Brainstorming literature connections is another effective application of SCAMPER. When you have a good book to share with your students but do not have specific ideas about how to use it, brainstorm with SCAMPER to produce several connections in just a few minutes. The Very Hungry Caterpillar is used as an example.

BOOK: The Very Hungry Caterpillar by Eric Carle

		Advanced Language	Analytical Thinking	Meaning Motivation	Perspective	Sense of Humor	Sensitivity	Accelerated Learning
S	**substitute:** Make up a funny story titled "The Very Hungry Tadpole."	•				•		
C	**combine:** What happens if the Very Hungry Caterpillar is following other caterpillars and they keep eating all the food before he gets to it? What does he say or do? How does he feel?			•	•	•		
A	**adapt:** Study real caterpillars, and retell the story so the Very Hungry Caterpillar only eats what real caterpillars eat.	•	•					
M	**modify:** Continue the story after the Very Hungry Caterpillar becomes a butterfly. Tell what happens next until a new egg is laid.	•	•					•
	minify: (Show the size of a caterpillar egg.) What hatches from eggs that are smaller? Tell a story about how the world appears to them.	•	•		•			•
	magnify: (Show the size of a caterpillar egg.) What hatches from eggs that are larger? Tell a story about how the world appears to them.	•	•		•			•
P	**put to other use:** Make figures out of felt, and retell the story on the flannel board.	•	•					
E	**eliminate:** Eliminate Saturday's food in the story. To continue the pattern established in the book, figure out what food item and how much of that item the Very Hungry Caterpillar should eat instead.			•				
R	**rearrange:** Research how long it takes caterpillars to get big enough to spin a chrysalis (not a cocoon). Rearrange the story to that length of time.		•	•				•
	reverse: Retell it by reversing the sequence.	•	•					

reverse: Retell it by reversing the sequence.

At the end, there was a beautiful butterfly.
Before the butterfly was a butterfly, it was a _____.
Before the chrysalis was a chrysalis, it was a _____.
Before the big caterpillar was a big caterpillar, it was a _____.
Before the little caterpillar was a caterpillar, it was a _____.
In the beginning, there was a little egg on a leaf.

Kingore, B. (2001). The Kingore Observation Inventory (KOI). 2nd ed. Austin: Professional Associates Publishing.

SCAMPER is an appropriate tool to use with older students when you increase the complexity of the generated questions. The open-ended format prompts high-level thinking and critical analysis in any subject area such as the balance of power in the government of the United States.

TOPIC: The Balance of Power

	Advanced Language	Analytical Thinking	Meaning Motivation	Perspective	Sense of Humor	Sensitivity	Accelerated Learning
S substitute: Describe how the balance of power would change if we had a monarch instead of a president?	•	•		•			
C combine: Describe what the effects would be if the President also served as the Chief Justice?	•	•	•	•			
A adapt: What other countries have a balance of power similar to the United States? Describe how do their systems differ. How do their systems affect the citizens of those countries?	•	•		•		•	•
M minify: If you could minify the power of Congress, which powers would you take away? How would the elected officials in Congress react to the changes? How might a citizen react?		•		•		•	
magnify: If you could increase the power of one of the governmental branches, which would it be? Explain what new control you would grant. Discuss who would most benefit from the changes.	•	•		•			
P put to other use: If you could alter the responsibilities of the President, what would you change? What are the advantages and disadvantages?		•		•			
E eliminate: If there could only be two branches of government, which would you eliminate to cause the least changes Americans' way of life?		•	•			•	•
R rearrange: In a speech before Congress, explain how you recommend changing the procedure for passing bills and making laws.	•	•					
reverse: Congress addresses new bills and determines if they should be passed, but the President has the power to veto their decisions. Explain what would change if that process was reversed.	•	•					•

Kingore, B. (2001). The Kingore Observation Inventory (KOI). 2nd ed. Austin: Professional Associates Publishing.

SCAMPER

BRAINSTORMING TOPIC

KOI CATEGORIES	Advanced Language	Analytical Thinking	Meaning Motivation	Perspective	Sense of Humor	Sensitivity	Accelerated Learning
S							
C							
A							
M							
P							
E							
R							

SCAMPER by Bob Eberie and Alex Osborn

Kingore, B. (2001). The Kingore Observation Inventory (KOI). 2nd ed. Austin: Professional Associates Publishing.

CHAPTER 6
Activities to
Nurture and Encourage Gifted Behaviors

In addition to the identification of students with gifted potentials, the categories of the KOI guide teachers' organization of enriched learning environments to nurture all students. Teachers focus on the responses of students and assess the categories in which they need to provide additional learning experiences that are challenging and nurturing.

Gifted behaviors seldom emerge on demand. It is ludicrous to think of any educator saying to a student: "Do something gifted--I'm watching and assessing!" Rather, teachers strive to take the top off of learning tasks by providing challenging experiences that are open-ended and invite high-level responses. Then, teachers observe how students respond and analyze which students demonstrate clues of gifted potentials or behaviors beyond the core curriculum expectations. However, caring teachers do not want to risk failure for some students in order to identify advanced potentials in others. Therefore, during assessment, learning experiences must be carefully planned so all students in the class are successful while some students bubble up to demonstrate behaviors that exceed expectations. After identification, a more rigorous curriculum should be integrated to match the readiness and needs of the identified gifted students.

This chapter includes multiple activities organized around the KOI categories. The purposes of the activities are to enable teachers to:
- Provide a variety of strategies and activities that students from diverse backgrounds can successfully complete on many different levels;
- Apply practical techniques and activities to stimulate thinking with less preparation time;
- Connect activities to a myriad of topics, content areas, and grade levels;
- Springboard discussions and more extensive topic responses;
- Celebrate diverse thinking by encouraging students to respond with multiple correct responses at different levels of understanding;
- Replace worksheet activities that require little thinking with active participation tasks that challenge students to generate responses; and
- Assess students' depth and complexity of content.

Kingore, B. (2001). <u>The Kingore Observation Inventory (KOI)</u>. 2nd ed. Austin: Professional Associates Publishing.

Grades	ADVANCED LANGUAGE

K - 8

1. Read Aloud

Read aloud daily to students. It enriches their vocabularies because "book talk" is not limited to the everyday words we use in oral communication. It enriches their background knowledge and literally gives them something to think about. "The single most important activity for building the knowledge required for eventual success in reading is reading aloud to children" (Anderson, et al., 1985).

K - 8

2. Word for the Week

Choose a new, enriching word to accent each week, such as "colleague" or "myriad". As a class, discuss it, use it in sentences, and try to role play or act it out. Encourage children to find ways to use that word in the classroom throughout the week. For concrete motivation, have a box of small, gold safety pins. Pin one on a student when you hear him/her correctly use the designated word. Try to build "chains of pins" by adding a pin to students' chains every time they use the designated word correctly and in a new manner.

K - 6

3. Fingerprint Art

Challenge students to think of ways to illustrate more advanced nouns with fingerprint art. Write the word on the bottom of a page. Let students use ink pads or markers to paint one finger and repeatedly make fingerprints to create an illustration for the word.

K - 8

4. Performances

Let small groups of students write and perform a short play, puppet show, or readers' theater for another class.

2 - 8

5. Word Visualization

Encourage students to write words in such a way that the visual representations illustrate what the words mean. Students can copy these on large index cards to organize in a card file. Challenge students to create word visualizations for every letter of the alphabet.

EXAMPLES:

  *petite*

2 - 6

6. ABC Sentences

Students write a sentence that is composed of words in alphabetical order. (Some use of connecting words such as conjunctions and articles is permitted.)

EXAMPLE: Alfred Bovine consumed daily eight fancy gumballs, hackleberry ice, jellied kisses, licorice, massive nuggets of peaches, quaint raisins, and seventeen turnips unabashed and valiantly without eXhibiting yawning zealously.

Kingore, B. (2001). The Kingore Observation Inventory (KOI). 2nd ed. Austin: Professional Associates Publishing.

4 - 8

7. Thesaurus Rewrites

Thesaurus Rewrites can be combined with written assignments to accent the enrichment of vocabularies and the use of strong words. However, the rewrites are most effective when a limited number of words are involved. Rewriting long text diminishes interest. The following are two activity examples.

1. When students complete any written assignment, have them circle two words then research and substitute more sophisticated or complex words.
2. Students use a thesaurus to rewrite short poems, first lines of songs, book titles, movie titles, or nursery rhymes. Ask others to read the rewrite and guess the original to add to the fun.

    EXAMPLES: "A Triplet of Ocular Deficient Rodents" for "Three Blind Mice"
    "Astonishing Lenience" for "Amazing Grace"

K - 8

8. Alphabet Time

Alphabet Time is a vocabulary and information organizer for any topic. Students think of the most significant things they know about the stated topic and list each word or fact by its beginning alphabet letter. Challenge students to get one or more responses for each letter.

- To model the process, make an overhead transparency of the Alphabet Time form in this chapter for the class or group to complete together. It also works well on large chart paper in primary classes.
- Alphabet Time is most effective when you do only a few letters each day. Completing the chart over several days encourages students to continue thinking about content.
- Record the initials of the student(s) who shared each idea. Noting credit often encourages more participation and high-level responses.
- The chart may be completed with single words, phrases, or sentences. Single words or phrases are effective to begin the process with young learners.
- After several experiences, students can use Alphabet Time to organize the results of independent study.

Alphabet Time

TOPIC: _Oceans_

A	nemone
B	lowfish; bay
C	oral reefs
D	olphins
E	el
F	ish
G	ray whale; gulf
H	urricanes
I	cebergs
J	ellyfish
K	elp
L	ionfish
M	anta ray
N	urse shark
O	ctopus
P	ollution
Q	uahog clams
R	usty shipwrecks
S	alt; sponges
T	renches; tide
U	nderwater vents
V	olcanos
W	aves
eX	tinction dangers
Y	ear-round fun
Z	ooplankton

4 - 8

9. Word Web

A Word Web requires in-depth exploration of word meanings. Using the form in this chapter, list a simple or complex verb or noun. Have students research synonyms, antonyms, and adverbs/adjectives. Then, students select their three best synonyms and antonyms to place appropriately on a continuum that denotes simple to more complex applications.

- Word Webs are most effective when completed in pairs or small groups to encourage discussions about word choices.
- When different groups work with the same word, post their completed Word Webs to invite a comparison of results and generate discussions.

Kingore, B. (2001). The Kingore Observation Inventory (KOI). 2nd ed. Austin: Professional Associates Publishing.

Alphabet Time

TOPIC: _Egypt_

A — _nything a pharaoh needed in the afterlife was…_
B — _uried with him in his tomb._
C — _anopic jars stored the stomach, liver, lungs, and intestines._
D — _iorite is the hard, black stone of many Egyptian sculptures._
E — _gypt is on the continent of Africa._
F — _lood water from the Nile River used to cover Egypt every spring._
G — _reat Pyramids are the tombs of Menkure, Khatre, and Khufu._
H — _ieroglyphics were the picture writings of ancient Egyptians._
I — _n Giza, the Great Pyramids…_
J — _uxtapose the desert sand._
K — _a was what Egyptians called their souls._
L — _imestone and granite were used to build the pyramids._
M — _ummification took 70 days and preserved the dead bodies._
N — _ecropolis was the city of the dead._
O — _nly priests and the pharaoh could go in the ritual chamber._
P — _apyrus was used to make paper._
Q — _uite a lot of ancient Egyptian structures are still standing._
R — _e was the sun god._
S — _arcophagi are the stone coffins._
T — _utankhamen was the famous, wealthy boy-king of Egypt._
U — _pper and Lower Egypt were united by King Narmer._
V — _otives were gifts made to the gods and goddesses._
W — _ater was channeled through the desert by the Egyptians._
X — _eric Egyptians made the desert their home and for many…_
Y — _ears they were a powerful culture._
Z — _illions of grains of sand cover Egypt._

Kingore, B. (2001). The Kingore Observation Inventory (KOI). 2nd ed. Austin: Professional Associates Publishing.

Word Web

DEFINITION ___1. to present voluntarily. 2. to place in the hands of. 3. to deliver___

USED IN A SENTENCE ___I will thoughtfully give you some of my ideas about___
___the problem.___

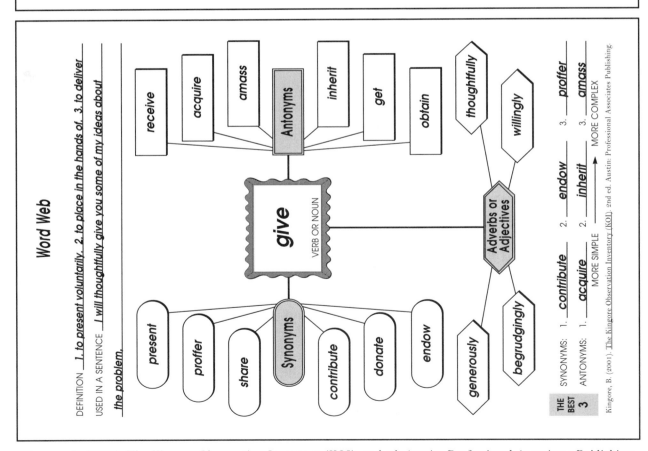

THE BEST 3	SYNONYMS:	1. ___contribute___	2. ___endow___	3. ___proffer___
	ANTONYMS:	1. ___acquire___	2. ___inherit___	3. ___amass___
		MORE SIMPLE ——→ MORE COMPLEX		

Kingore, B. (2001). The Kingore Observation Inventory (KOI). 2nd ed. Austin: Professional Associates Publishing.

Kingore, B. (2001). The Kingore Observation Inventory (KOI). 2nd ed. Austin: Professional Associates Publishing.

Alphabet Time

TOPIC: _____

A
B
C
D
E
F
G
H
I
J
K
L
M
N
O
P
Q
R
S
T
U
V
W
X
Y
Z

_____
_____
_____
_____
_____
_____
_____
_____
_____
_____
_____
_____
_____
_____
_____
_____
_____
_____
_____
_____
_____
_____
_____
_____
_____
_____

Kingore, B. (2001). <u>The Kingore Observation Inventory (KOI)</u>. 2nd ed. Austin: Professional Associates Publishing.

Word Web

DEFINITION _____

USED IN A SENTENCE _____

_____

Synonyms

VERB OR NOUN

Antonyms

Adverbs or Adjectives

SYNONYMS: 1. _____   2. _____   3. _____

ANTONYMS: 1. _____   2. _____   3. _____

MORE SIMPLE ——————→ MORE COMPLEX

Kingore, B. (2001). The Kingore Observation Inventory (KOI). 2nd ed. Austin: Professional Associates Publishing.

Grades | **ANALYTICAL THINKING**

K - 5

1. Roll Call Learning

Call student's names and ask for different responses relating to the current topic.

> Say: "When I call your name, answer with..."
> * Your last name
> * Your favorite smell (or any sense)
> * An animal that lives in rainforrests
> * Something that has two legs/four legs/wings/a beak
> * Something made of wood/metal/leather/cotton/plastic/glass
> * Something that is oval (or any shape)
> * A number greater than _____ (less than _____)
> * Something a magnet attracts
> * A three-syllable word
> * One attribute of _____

Encourage students to listen to each other and think of a different response each time. This process is also useful when you need to call children to get in line, get wraps, wait for others to finish, at transition times, or when a change of pace is needed during a lesson.

K - 8

2. Venn Diagrams

Present intersecting circles, and encourage students to list three or more similarities and differences between two things. Increase complex thinking by intersecting three circles in order to compare and contrast multiple aspects of a topic, such as three different environments, historical figures, or mathematical operations.

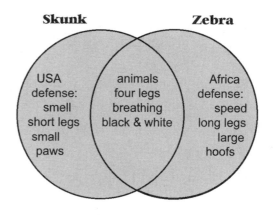

K - 8

3. Graphing

Use bar, line, and pie graphs for the students to organize data. In primary grades, graph the colors worn by the students, favorite TV shows or foods, number of people in each family, and other variables. Upper grade levels also graph percentages, probability studies, and the results from scientific observations or experiments.

Human graphs are also fun. Lay pictures or objects representing the subject for graphing, such as the colors of the rainbow, in a line on the floor. Each student selects a favorite or most appropriate choice and stands in a line in front of that one. Count and discuss the results of the three-dimensional graph.

Kingore, B. (2001). <u>The Kingore Observation Inventory (KOI)</u>. 2nd ed. Austin: Professional Associates Publishing.

K – 8

4. Webbing/Mapping Relationships

Have children show the relationships of the various aspects of a topic by doing a webbing activity. Start with the key term in the center, and draw lines to connect related words/ideas. As a variation, students draw around their hand to use as a webbing format to organize main idea/details, topic/facts, topic/attributes, or story/events.

hunting shelter

far North   ice blocks

IGLOO

below freezing   Eskimo

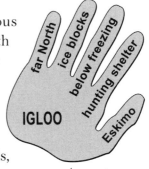

far North
ice blocks
below freezing
hunting shelter
IGLOO
Eskimo

1 – 8

5. Number Challenge

The Number Challenge combines mathematical operations with logic. Students play in pairs to reach a predetermined total using the procedures and operations described on the following page. To prepare a Number Challenge board, write numbers on the blank game form in this section, or have students draw their own shapes to create unique playing boards. Change the combinations of numbers to those most appropriate for the designated total of each game.

The greatest analysis results when students must determine for themselves which numbers to record on a game board for a specific total before they play the game. Having pairs of students write their own number combinations ensures different playing boards instead of all games being the same.

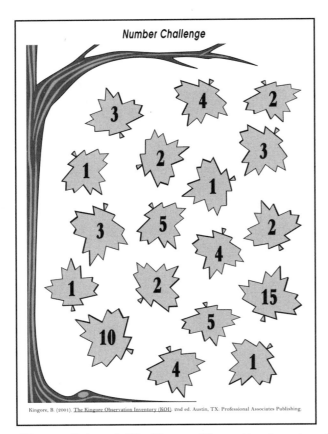

Number Challenge

3 4 2 2 3 1 2 1 3 5 2 4 1 2 15 10 5 4 1

Kingore, B. (2001). The Kingore Observation Inventory (KOI). 2nd ed. Austin, TX: Professional Associates Publishing.

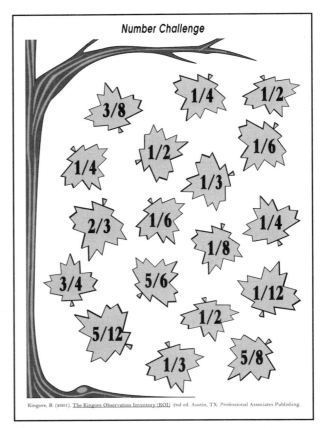

Number Challenge

3/8 1/4 1/2 1/2 1/6 1/4 1/3 2/3 1/6 1/4 1/8 3/4 5/6 1/12 5/12 1/2 1/3 5/8

Kingore, B. (2001). The Kingore Observation Inventory (KOI). 2nd ed. Austin, TX: Professional Associates Publishing.

Kingore, B. (2001). The Kingore Observation Inventory (KOI). 2nd ed. Austin: Professional Associates Publishing.

Procedure for Addition

After determining the number challenge objective, e.g., 27, the first player selects one number and covers it with a scrap of paper. The second player selects and covers the next number and adds the two selected numbers together. Continue taking turns, each time adding the selected number to the combined total. The winner is the first person to reach the game objective, e.g., 27.

Procedure for Subtraction

With the number challenge determined, e.g., 27, each player takes turns selecting numbers to subtract from 27. The winner is the first to reach 0.

Procedure for Multiplication

Use a large number for the number challenge, e.g., 1800. The first player covers one number on the board. Each player in turn selects a number to multiply by the previous amount. The winner is the player who comes the closest without going over the game objective, e.g., 1800.

Procedure for Division

Begin with a large number, e.g., 1800. Each selected number is used to divide the previous amount. The winner is the player who reaches the smallest positive number possible.

Variations

- Use fractions or decimals instead of whole numbers.
- Allow students to combine different operations as they play.
- Have students plan together the greatest/smallest number of turns that could be used.

2 - 8

6. How Do You and the Character Compare?

Challenge students to analyze how they compare to one of the characters in a book. The form on page 87 encourages them to use graphics and words in their comparison.

4 - 8

7. Logic Problems

After experiences with logic problems and grids, differentiate the curriculum by having the students create their own logic problems that relate to the content being studied. Typically, more analysis is required when students create their own product examples than when they complete the examples of others.

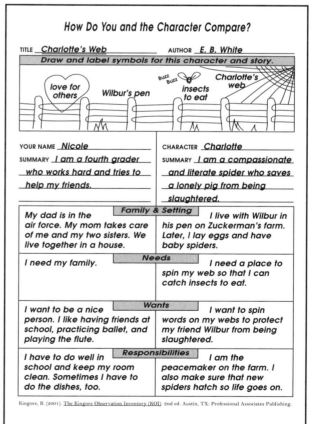

How Do You and the Character Compare?

TITLE _Charlotte's Web_   AUTHOR _E. B. White_

Draw and label symbols for this character and story.

love for others   Wilbur's pen   Buzz Buzz insects to eat   Charlotte's web

YOUR NAME _Nicole_
SUMMARY _I am a fourth grader who works hard and tries to help my friends._

CHARACTER _Charlotte_
SUMMARY _I am a compassionate and literate spider who saves a lonely pig from being slaughtered._

Family & Setting
My dad is in the air force. My mom takes care of me and my two sisters. We live together in a house.
I live with Wilbur in his pen on Zuckerman's farm. Later, I lay eggs and have baby spiders.

Needs
I need my family.
I need a place to spin my web so that I can catch insects to eat.

Wants
I want to be a nice person. I like having friends at school, practicing ballet, and playing the flute.
I want to spin words on my webs to protect my friend Wilbur from being slaughtered.

Responsibilities
I have to do well in school and keep my room clean. Sometimes I have to do the dishes, too.
I am the peacemaker on the farm. I also make sure that new spiders hatch so life goes on.

Kingore, B. (2001). The Kingore Observation Inventory (KOI). 2nd ed. Austin, TX: Professional Associates Publishing.

Kingore, B. (2001). <u>The Kingore Observation Inventory (KOI)</u>. 2nd ed. Austin: Professional Associates Publishing.

Number Challenge

Kingore, B. (2001). <u>The Kingore Observation Inventory (KOI)</u>. 2nd ed. Austin: Professional Associates Publishing.

How Do You and the Character Compare?

TITLE_____ AUTHOR_____

Draw and label symbols for this character and story.

YOUR NAME_____ CHARACTER_____

SUMMARY _____ SUMMARY _____

_____ _____

_____ _____

_____ _____

	Family & Setting	
	Needs	
	Wants	
	Responsibilities	

Kingore, B. (2001). <u>The Kingore Observation Inventory (KOI)</u>. 2nd ed. Austin: Professional Associates Publishing.

Grades	MEANING MOTIVATION

K - 4

1. Mother Goose Interviews

Together, brainstorm questions to ask if interviewing nursery rhyme characters. Let individuals or pairs of students write how a specific character might answer each question. Then, the children share their answers aloud and challenge others to figure out each character or rhyme. The same process may be repeated later for folk and fairy tale characters.

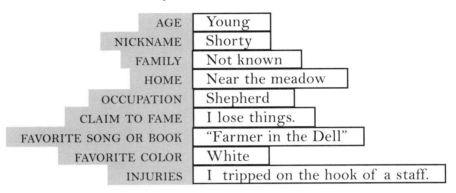

AGE	Young
NICKNAME	Shorty
FAMILY	Not known
HOME	Near the meadow
OCCUPATION	Shepherd
CLAIM TO FAME	I lose things.
FAVORITE SONG OR BOOK	"Farmer in the Dell"
FAVORITE COLOR	White
INJURIES	I tripped on the hook of a staff.

(Rhyme: Little Bo Peep)

K - 6

2. Research Flap Books

After teaching students how to fold and cut flap books, let them use the format to share their research on a topic of their interest. The outside of a flap can contain an interesting question, and the answer is revealed when the flap is lifted. Encourage students to note the resources used and to seek in-depth information rather than simple facts.

Directions for Making Flap Books

a. Fold a piece of paper lengthwise (hotdog fold) and widthwise (hamburger fold).

b. Unfold the paper leaving it divided into fourths.

c. Cut along one of the folds to the center of the paper. If the crease along the hotdog fold is cut, the book will be taller. If the crease along the hamburger fold is cut, the book will be wider.

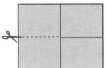

d. Fold the paper in half making two flaps, each a quarter-size of the paper.

e. Close the paper so that the two flaps are on the inside facing each other.

f. Repeat steps a through e with another piece of paper.

g. Glue the outside-back of one flap page to the outside-front of another. This will create the look of a book with a flap on each page. Continue connecting flap pages to reach your preferred book length. Decorate the outside cover, and include the book title and author.

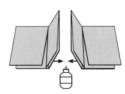

Adapted from: Literature Celebrations (Kingore, 1999).

Kingore, B. (2001). The Kingore Observation Inventory (KOI). 2nd ed. Austin: Professional Associates Publishing.

K - 8

3. Wonder-Full

"Wonder-Full", a poem by Kathy Hall, demonstrates the questioning attitude typical of bright students. A blank frame of the poem is provided on page 92 for students to communicate their wonderments. Consider using the blank form as a focus activity when introducing a topic. Primary students, working as a class or in small groups, orally suggest questions for the teacher to record before they begin a unit. Challenge older students to individually complete the form and organize questions they generate about the topic. Also, use the form as a precursor to individual research.

K - 8

4. Question Quest

As a focus activity, students generate as many questions as they can about a given topic. Encourage speculative questions, such as "What if...?", "Has anyone ever...?", and "Why...?" Many questions may not have an answer but rather deal with the issues related to the topic. Revisit and discuss the questions as the topic is studied.

K - 8

5. Wordless Books

Let students construct meaning by writing the storyline for a wordless book. Wordless books encourage students to connect their schema to the ideas of the author. The results celebrate diversity as different text versions of the same story are produced. Several examples of wordless books are included in the Meaning Motivation section of the Annotated Bibliography. Some titles such as Pancakes for Breakfast and Changes, Changes are very appealing to primary writers. Other titles such as Windows and Sector 7 are complex enough to appeal to mature and philosophical thinkers.

K - 8

6. "What If" in Science

Write five "what if" or unanswered questions pertaining to science. Which one would be most interesting to research further? Why?

Wonder-Full

I wonder how sunsets change colors.
What makes them glow so?
Why are they red?

I wonder if Mars could be lived on.
How would we get there?
Could we come back?

I wonder who first thought of money.
What was it made of?
What did it buy?

I wonder what's after the universe.
What could be out there?
How would it look?

I wonder when we'll heal our planet.
How could we do it?
What will we need?

I wonder why I always wonder.
Why do I want to know...
How?
If?
Who?
What?
When?
Why?

Kathy Hall

Kingore, B. (2001). The Kingore Observation Inventory (KOI). 2nd ed. Austin: Professional Associates Publishing.

K – 8

7. Do-Not-Disturb Times

Periodically, provide times when students can elect to pursue in-depth investigations of a school-appropriate area of interest. These investigations can serve as replacement activities for a skill or topic for which a student has demonstrated mastery in preassessment tasks.

Variations
*   Require students to set goals to help clarify the focus and organization of their investigations. Assessment: Time Saving Procedures for Busy Teachers (Kingore, 1999) has several simplified goal-setting forms that are applicable.
*   Build in periodic checkpoints at which students share with others what they have learned and which questions they continue to research. Encourage appropriate feedback and suggestions from the audience.

2 – 8

8. Question that Number

Provide a math story problem with the task statement or question omitted. Students work in pairs to write questions that explain each possible answer in a multiple-choice format.

> *A mailman delivered 12 packages and 27 letters. Then, he delivered 11 special delivery folders. Another mailman delivered 7 special delivery folders to an office building and 126 pen pal letters to a school.*
>
> *What is the question if the answer is:*
> ☐ *183*   ☐ *99*   ☐ *4*
> ☐ *50*   ☐ *133*

3 – 8

9. Question That! (A Bulletin Board)

Question That! is an interactive bulletin board inviting students to think and question. Prepare the board by using a light-colored backing and adding a border. Then, as the example on the next page illustrates, use yarn with a stapler or different colors of construction paper to divide the board into boxes, enough for the number of students in the class or in one section. Put one student's name in each box, and add a caption at the top of the board.

Post a different answer each day. Every student writes an appropriate question that has that answer and places it on the board by his or her name. Encourage thoughtful questions that extend beyond the simple or obvious.

Connect the activity to a topic of study by using concept words, terminology, locations, or people related to that topic. Students typically want to compare and discuss questions on the board.

Variations
*   Specify the content, and let pairs of students take turns determining and posting a different answer each day for the others to question.
*   See how many different questions students can write in two minutes.

Kingore, B. (2001). The Kingore Observation Inventory (KOI). 2nd ed. Austin: Professional Associates Publishing.

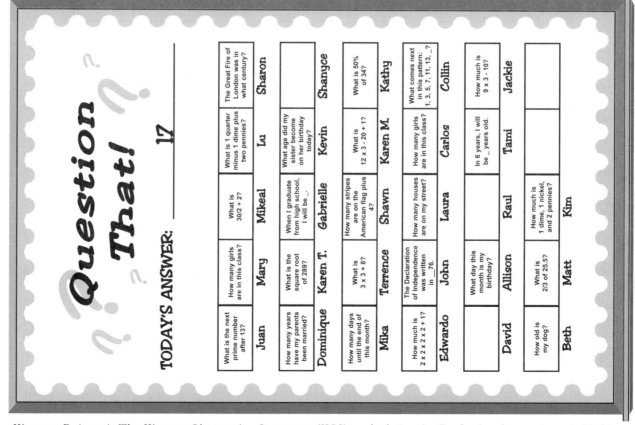

Wonder-Full

I wonder how   photosynthesis works   .   ?
How do chloroplasts use solar energy   ?
What do the chloroplasts do when there is no sunlight   ?

I wonder if   the changing atmosphere will affect plants   .   ?
Will chloroplasts utilize more radiation   ?
Does pollution block solar energy from chloroplasts   ?

I wonder who   discovered chloroplasts in plant cells   ?
Who was the first person to think to use solar energy   ✓
the way plants do   ?

I wonder what   transfers the energy from chloroplasts   ?
What controls the spread of energy throughout the plant   ?
What do trees do in the winter when they have no leaves   ?

I wonder when   chloroplasts start working in a new cell   .
Do old cells ever make new chloroplasts   ?
How do plants produce chloroplasts in the cells   ?

I wonder why   chloroplasts are only green   .
Why do they reflect the green light and not use it too   ?
Did plants use different light millions of years ago   ?

I wonder!

Adapted form the poem, "Wonder-Full," by Kathy Hall
Used with permission.

Kingore, B. (2001). The Kingore Observation Inventory (KOI). 2nd ed. Austin, TX: Professional Associates Publishing.

Question That!

TODAY'S ANSWER: _____ 17

What is the next prime number after 13?	How many girls are in this class?	What is 30/2 + 2?	What is 1 quarter minus 1 dime plus two pennies?	The Great Fire of London was in what century?
Juan	Mary	Mikeal	Lu	Sharon
How many years have my parents been married?	What is the square root of 289?	When I graduate from high school, I will be __.	What age did my sister become on her birthday today?	
Dominique	Karen T.	Gabrielle	Kevin	Shanyce
How many days until the end of this month?	What is 3 x 3 + 8?	How many stripes are on the American flag plus 4?	What is 12 x 3 - 20 + 1?	What is 50% of 34?
Mika	Terrence	Shawn	Karen M.	Kathy
How much is 2 x 2 x 2 x 2 + 1?	The Declaration of Independence was written in __76.	How many houses are on my street?	How many girls are in this class?	What comes next in this pattern: 1, 3, 5, 7, 11, 13, __?
Edwardo	John	Laura	Carlos	Collin
	What day this month is my birthday?		In 6 years, I will be __ years old.	How much is 9 x 3 - 10?
David	Allison	Raul	Tami	Jackie
How old is my dog?	What is 2/3 of 25.5?	How much is 1 dime, 1 nickel, and 2 pennies?		
Beth	Matt	Kim		

Kingore, B. (2001). The Kingore Observation Inventory (KOI). 2nd ed. Austin: Professional Associates Publishing.

Wonder-Full

I wonder how _____ .
_____ ?
_____ ?

I wonder if _____ .
_____ ?
_____ ?

I wonder who _____ .
_____ ?
_____ ?

I wonder what _____ .
_____ ?
_____ ?

I wonder when _____ .
_____ ?
_____ ?

I wonder why _____ .
_____ ?
_____ ?

I wonder!

Adapted form the poem, "Wonder-Full," by Kathy Hall
Used with permission.

Kingore, B. (2001). The Kingore Observation Inventory (KOI). 2nd ed. Austin: Professional Associates Publishing.

Grades	*PERSPECTIVE*

K - 3

1. Hole-Reinforcer Art

Provide a number of hole reinforcers for each student to attach to a blank paper. Then, students draw a picture incorporating the reinforcers as part of the illustration. Encourage students to write or tell about their picture.

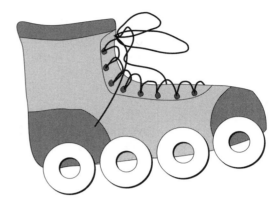

I wish I had roller blades! My mom thinks they are too dangerous.

Variations

• Students make number concept books by using a different number of reinforcers on each page to incorporate into pictures.

• Provide self-adhesive, colored dots (they are sold as color-coding labels in office supply stores) to use instead of reinforcers as the picture prompts.

• As a class, graph how many different ideas students came up with using the same number of reinforcers or dots. Accent the value of original ideas, and encourage students to feel more comfortable about moving beyond the obvious.

K - 5

2. Blueprints

After viewing examples of architecture blueprints, students draw a floorplan of the school, their classroom, their home, or their room at home.

K - 5

3. Turn About Figures

In Beau Gardiner's The Turn About, Think About, Look About Book., every illustration becomes something different when viewed from the top, bottom, or either side of the page. The illustrations in Ann Jonas' Round Trip becomes completely different pictures when viewed upsidedown. Share these books as background visual information. Then, let children draw geometric figures on their papers and see how many different illustrations they can create for each view as they turn the paper.

K - 5

4. Fairy Tales

Read several traditional and contemporary versions of the same fairy tale. Many have very different events and endings that reflect, in part, the amount of humor or violence each author felt appropriate. Discuss the differences in the way each author chose to tell the story and why the author might have made that choice.

Kingore, B. (2001). The Kingore Observation Inventory (KOI). 2nd ed. Austin: Professional Associates Publishing.

K - 6   **5. Draw Starts**

Draw Starts are incomplete drawings used to prompt students' perspective and analysis. Any simple graphic on a paper can be a Draw Start. Four examples are shared on page 96. Each of these is meant to be enlarged on one page by itself to allow room for students to draw and write.

Draw Starts can be used in any general way to motivate students' imagination and encourage diverse ideas. However, they can also relate to content by specifying a category for the drawing. The following suggestions are intended to prompt more ideas for using Draw Starts with instructional topics.

Multiple Perspectives
Analyze a draw start from multiple perspectives by turning the paper. Draw and write a different response for all four sides of the paper.

Language Arts
1. Use one or more letters of the alphabet as a Draw Start.
2. Use one or more punctuation marks as a Draw Start.
3. People use this to communicate or record ideas.
4. This is part of an important message.
5. This is the setting of the story.
6. This is part of a significant event in the story.
7. The main character could use this to solve the problem.

Math
1. Use one or more numerals as a Draw Start.
2. Use one or more geometric shapes as a Draw Start.
3. Use one or more math symbols as a Draw Start.
4. This exists in even numbers.
5. This is related to a prime number.
6. This is one way math is used at home.
7. People use math to plan how to make this.
8. This illustrates fractions in a common item.

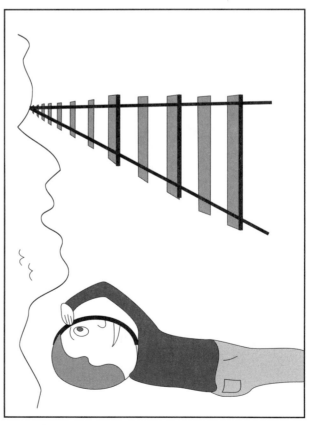

Kingore, B. (2001). <u>The Kingore Observation Inventory (KOI)</u>. 2nd ed. Austin: Professional Associates Publishing.

Science

1. Use one or more pieces of scientific equipment as a Draw Start, e.g., a magnet or test tube.
2. This is important to people's health.
3. This is a way science is used at home.
4. This is something that lives underground/underwater/in the air.
5. This is found in a rain forest.
6. Dinosaurs needed this to survive.
7. This is a carnivore/herbivore/omnivore.
8. This grows and likes sunshine.
9. In an amusement park, this illustrates the scientific principle of _____.

Social Studies

1. Use the shape of one or more states/countries as a Draw Start.
2. Use a state flag or another state symbol as a Draw Start.
3. This helps bring people together.
4. This is important in my life.
5. Friends do this together.
6. This is a kind of transportation.
7. This played a major role in the history of the United States.
8. This is only found in rural areas/a foreign country/another continent.

K - 8
6. Perspective Switch

Students work in small groups or individually to rewrite a well-known story or folk tale from the point-of-view of another character.

K - 8
7. Perspective Map

In the center frame, draw and/or write about a scene or object related to the current topic of study. Then, prompt multiple perspectives by brainstorming what different people, places, or things might think about that scene or object and writing them in the thought clouds.

Kingore, B. (2000). The Kingore Observation Inventory (KOI). 2nd ed. Austin, TX: Professional Associates Publishing.

Kingore, B. (2001). The Kingore Observation Inventory (KOI). 2nd ed. Austin: Professional Associates Publishing.

Draw Starts

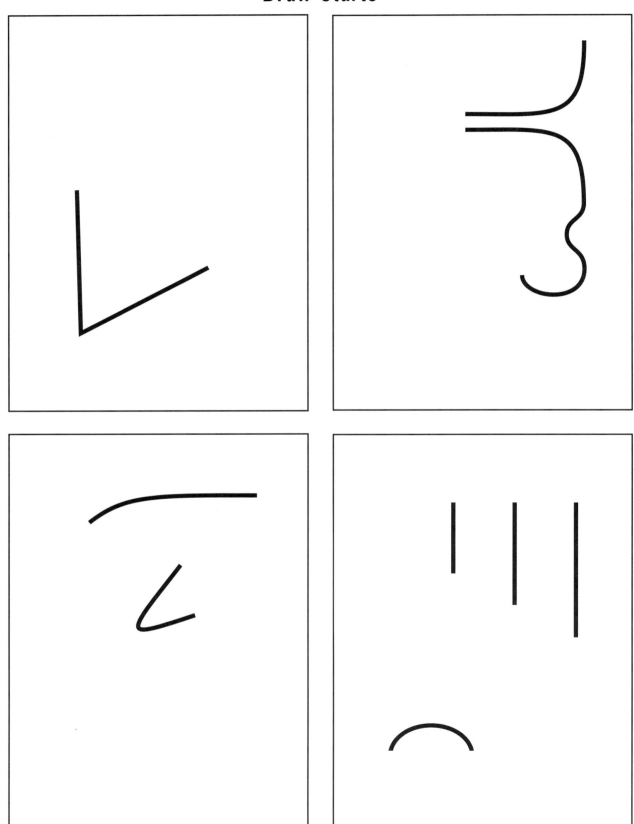

Kingore, B. (2001). The Kingore Observation Inventory (KOI). 2nd ed. Austin: Professional Associates Publishing.

Perspective Map

Kingore, B. (2001). <u>The Kingore Observation Inventory (KOI)</u>. 2nd ed. Austin: Professional Associates Publishing.

Grades	SENSE OF HUMOR

K - 3

1. Topic Captions

Provide topic-related pictures, or let children cut out interesting, topic-related pictures from magazines. Then, children create humorous captions for the pictures. Invite comparisons and discussions by posting multiple captions for the same picture.

K - 5

2. Sunday Comics

Cut out or white out some of the speech balloons from students' favorite Sunday comic strips. Encourage students to write their own versions of the characters' conversations.

K - 6

3. Hink Pinks, Hinky Pinkys, and Hinkadink Pinkadinks

Hink Pinks are riddles with two-word, rhyming answers; each word in the answer has only one syllable. For example, a happy father is a "glad dad" and the best police officer is a "top cop". To create Hink Pinks, students brainstorm rhyming, one-syllable words, and then, they create a riddle for each to share with others in a question and answer format.

> EXAMPLE: What do you call an angry lima?
> ANSWER: A mean bean
> EXAMPLE: What grows in a fragile yard?
> ANSWER: Glass grass

Continue the rhyming fun by composing a Hinky Pinky with a two-syllable rhyming answer.

> EXAMPLE: What do you call a wet hound?
> ANSWER: A soggy doggy
> EXAMPLE: What is the flaking top of a room?
> ANSWER: A peeling ceiling

Increase the complexity with a Hinkadink Pinkadink riddle that has a three-syllable rhyming answer.

> EXAMPLE: What yellow fruit grows in Cuba?
> ANSWER: A Havana banana
> EXAMPLE: What is the White House?
> ANSWER: The President's residence

Challenge older students to attempt four-syllable rhymes and create their own name for the results.

K - 8

4. Fractured Tales

Model fractured tales with a collection of pictures or symbols from various folk tales. Start retelling a familiar folk tale as you hold up or point to a related picture. In the middle of an idea, switch folk tales but continue the same story line. After a while, switch again as in the following example.

Kingore, B. (2001). The Kingore Observation Inventory (KOI). 2nd ed. Austin: Professional Associates Publishing.

Once upon a time, an adventurous little girl named Goldilocks decided to go for a walk in the woods. When she came to a house and peeked in the window, she saw pigs dancing. She knocked at the door. "Let me come in!" she said. "Not by the hair on our chinny chin chins!" said the pigs. While Goldilocks was at the pigs' door, a giant troll saw her and said, "I'm going to eat you up!" Goldilocks pushed open the door, ran inside, and slammed it just in time. Then, the troll heard, "Run, run, run as fast as you can! You can't catch me I'm the gingerbread man!" The troll chased the gingerbread man until he became too tired and went back under his bridge to rest.

Next, students write or tell their own versions of fractured tales. Use the activity as a review technique to revisit many of the characters and events from books read by the class.

K - 8 5. Animal Cartoons

Invite students to create original animal comic characters and then draw a speech balloon beside the creation. Students dictate a response or write in the speech balloon to respond to the content being studied. Students can use their own art ideas, or encourage students less satisfied with their own drawing to select examples from the Animal Cartoons on page 102 to combine and create a funny animal.

1 - 8 6. Book of Flip Strips

Teach students how to fold and cut a Book of Flip Strips from the directions on the following page. With younger students, make two flip strips for each page instead of three. Older students can expand the book to four strips for increased complexity.

Show students how to mark short lines on each piece so the connecting parts of the drawings will line up on each strip after being cut. Then, students draw different segments of people or animals on each flip strip to create humorous combinations when different flip strips are turned.

For older students, connect this activity to content by developing Books of Flip Strips that incorporate words and illustrations to compare different animals, stories, historical figures, or concepts being studied. For example, when studying oceans, the tops strips can be used for discussing and illustrating plant life, the middle for animal life, and the bottom for geographic features. Different pages then compare appearances, attributes, development, etc.

As another variation, turn the book horizontally and print prefixes, roots, and suffixes on each strip.

Kingore, B. (2001). <u>The Kingore Observation Inventory (KOI)</u>. 2nd ed. Austin: Professional Associates Publishing.

Directions for Making a Book of Flip Strips

a. Line up the number of sheets that will comprise the inside pages of the book.

b. Fold those pieces of paper into the desired number of strips. Fold all of them at the same time so that the strips will be the same size and turn easily when the book is completed.

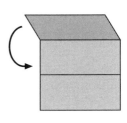

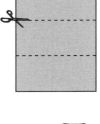

c. Cut each page along the folds keeping the top, middle, and bottom pieces in order. Then, if their sizes vary somewhat, the strips will still flip well.

d. Align the strips from top to bottom, and lay them on an uncut piece of paper. This paper becomes the back cover. Place another piece of uncut paper on top of the strips for the front cover.

e. Staple the book six times on the left side (two for each strip) to secure the book.

f. After the blank books are stapled together, draw and write on each strip to organize the contents of the book.

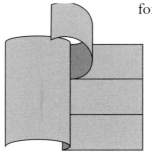

FINISHED PRODUCT

1 - 8

7. **Partial Proverbs**

Present only the first half of proverbs or famous quotations. Students write their versions to complete the sayings. Some students enjoy illustrating their creations. (The Flap Book described in the Meaning Motivation section of this chapter is an effective product for this activity.) Post the finished versions for everyone to read.

> ***The following are examples of proverb conclusions written by first, second, and third graders.***
>
> A bird in the hand... is messy.
>
> Don't count your chickens before... morning because it's too dark outside.
>
> The early bird gets... to wait in the cafeteria.
>
> You can't teach an old dog new... manners.
>
> An apple a day... is good for the store's business.

Variations

*   Use quotations related to historical events being studied.
*   Use proverbs that relate to themes of the books read by the class.
*   For a specific quotation, research the person quoted and the context of that statement.

Kingore, B. (2001). The Kingore Observation Inventory (KOI). 2nd ed. Austin: Professional Associates Publishing.

2 - 8

8. Cartoon Captions

Cut the captions from single frame cartoons, and ask students to create humorous new captions. For a surprising variation, post an empty frame as a blank cartoon, and let students write multiple captions for the invisible cartoon. Finally, students draw their own cartoons and write one or more captions for them.

Caption: _____
_____

Possible Captions:

"The Invisible Man"
"Snow White"
"It Looked Like Spilt Milk"
"Square Not"
"Gone!"
"Head in the Clouds"

2 - 8

9. Laughing Out Loud (A Bulletin Board)

Laughing Out Loud is an interactive bulletin board inviting students to research, use bibliographic references, and understand a potential audience. Cover a bulletin board with a light-colored background. Add a border that coordinates with your other room decorations, and put the title "Laughing Out Loud" at the top of the bulletin board. Provide an assortment of books containing jokes, riddles, cartoons, and word plays. On the floor under the bulletin board, place a few large pillows that invite students to sit or lie on the floor and read the books.

Students research to find the joke, riddle, etc. that they think the class will find the most amusing. Then, they use brightly colored markers to write that humorous item graffiti-style on the bulletin board paper. Under the item, students write the bibliographic reference so others can locate the original source and read more items from it.

Laughing Out Loud!

First Baseman: What did the umpire do when the count was full?
Second Baseman: Burp him!
Christopher, Matt. <u>Baseball Jokes and Riddles</u>. Boston: Little, Brown, & Co. 1996.

MARK: What state is round at both ends and high in the middle?
RYAN: Who knows?
MARK: Ohio.
Phillips, Bob. <u>Awesome Good Clean Jokes for Kids</u>. Eugene, Oregon: Harvest House. 1992.

Sign in a shoe store window: COME IN AND HAVE A FIT
Rosenbloom, Joseph. <u>The Gigantic Joke Book</u>. New York: Sterling. 1978.

Moe: I've been seeing spots before my eyes lately.
Joe: Have you seen a doctor?
Moe: No, just spots.
Rosenbloom, Joseph. <u>The Gigantic Joke Book</u>. New York: Sterling. 1978.

--Waiter, this egg is bad.
--Don't blame me ma'am, I only laid the table.
Archbold, Tim. <u>Ha! Ha! Ha!</u> New York: King Fisher. 1999.

Knock, Knock.
Who's there?
Howie.
Howie who?
I'm okay, how are you?
Rosenbloom, Joseph. <u>Doctor Knock Knock's Official Knock-Knock Dictionary</u>. New York: Sterling. 1976.

Ernie: I just swallowed a bone.
Bernie: Are you choaking?
Ernie: No, I'm serious.
Rosenbloom, Joseph. <u>The Gigantic Joke Book</u>. New York: Sterling. 1978.

TEACHER: What does "coincidence" mean?
TRACY: Funny, I was just about to ask you that.
Rosenbloom, Joseph. <u>696 Silly School Jokes and Riddles</u>. New York: Sterling. 1986.

Kingore, B. (2001). <u>The Kingore Observation Inventory (KOI)</u>. 2nd ed. Austin: Professional Associates Publishing.

Animal Cartoons

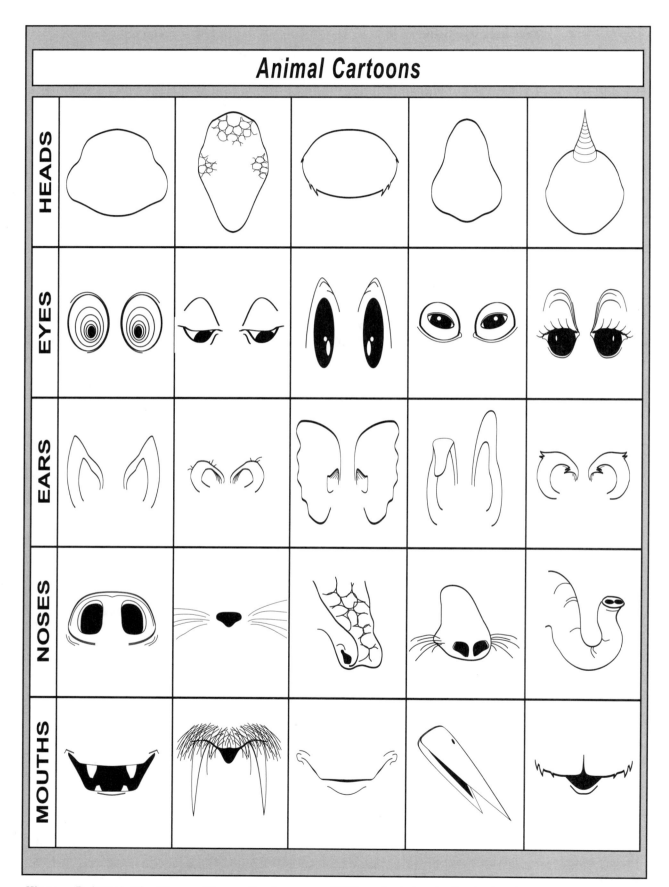

Kingore, B. (2001). <u>The Kingore Observation Inventory (KOI)</u>. 2nd ed. Austin: Professional Associates Publishing.

Grades	SENSITIVITY

K - 3

1. Sensitive Artists

Children illustrate scenes of people helping others or what a story character should do to be fair. They then tell or write about the illustrations.

K - 5

2. ME and WE

Provide opportunities for the children to reflect and write about themselves as individuals or as members of groups. Kindergartners can write or dictate their responses to the teacher or to big buddies from an older class. Begin with prompts such as the following.

- I am _____.
- I am good at _____.
- I am not good at _____.
- I like _____.
- I do not like _____.
- I want to be _____.
- I wish _____.
- I do not want _____.
- I feel _____.

- We are _____.
- We are good at _____.
- We are not good at _____.
- We like _____.
- We do not like _____.
- We want to be _____.
- We wish _____.
- We do not want _____.
- We feel _____.

A ME form and a WE form for children to complete is included on pages 106 and 107. For added emphasis and interest, duplicate the forms back to back on a piece of paper. Children write and tell about themselves; then, they flip the paper over to write and tell about being with others, such as "Me" and "My Family" or "Me" and "My Class".

K - 8

3. Personal Analogies

A personal analogy is a metaphorical form describing a person's feelings or empathetic identification with a concept, plant, animal, or non-living thing. Analogies can be simple or complex such as the following.

> EXAMPLE OF FEELING:
> *I am like a lighthouse when I reach out to help others who are in rocky situations.*
>
> EXAMPLE OF EMPATHIC IDENTITY:
> *I am a lighthouse, alone but standing strong.*

Provide sentence stems that prompt students to make personal analogies. Connect the activity to content by comparing people to topical items of study. Many students enjoy writing a content-related analogy and illustrating it.

- If I were an animal, I would be a _____ because _____.
- I am like a _____ living in a rainforest because _____.
- I am like the catylist in this science experiment when _____.

Kingore, B. (2001). The Kingore Observation Inventory (KOI). 2nd ed. Austin: Professional Associates Publishing.

- When I'm with people, I'm like a _____ because _____.
- When I'm by myself, I'm like a _____ because _____.

If I was an animal I would be a sloth because they are very lazy like I am.

by Robin

K - 8

4. Make a Difference

Encourage students to experience the great feeling of accomplishing something that helps others. Plan ways in which students have the power and resources to make a difference. Inspire others, and organize their assistance in a project such as an anti-litter campaign with TV news coverage or a read-aloud and writing-partners program to help younger learners.

Here are some ways to help the school, community, or world.

1. Volunteer. Donate time and energy to tutor, clean up an area, or visit people in need.
2. Raise money for charities through car washes, pledges for a walk-a-thon, or recycling collections.
3. Write letters to express feelings and insights needed for changes.

Communicate with local groups to determine ways to help, or contact national organizations such as the few listed below.

BOYS & GIRLS CLUBS OF AMERICA	HABITAT FOR HUMANITY
1230 W. Peachtree Street, NW Atlanta, GA 30309 404/815-5700 www.bgca.com	121 Habitat Street Americus, GA 31709-3498 229/924-6935 www.habitat.org
MARCH OF DIMES	NATIONAL WILDLIFE FEDERATION
1275 Mamaroneck Avenue White Plains, NY 10605 888/663-4637 www.modimes.org	8925 Leesburg Pike Vienna, VA 22184 703/790-4000 www.nwf.org
RAINFOREST ALLIANCE	YOUNG AMERICA CARES! (YAC!)
65 Bleecker Street New York, NY 10012 888-MY EARTH www.rainforest-alliance.org	701 N. Fairfax Street Alexandria, VA 22314 703/836-7100 (ext. 445) www.unitedway.org

Kingore, B. (2001). The Kingore Observation Inventory (KOI). 2nd ed. Austin: Professional Associates Publishing.

1 - 6

5. Thinking About _____.

Provide the Thinking About form on page 108 for students to draw and write about an item, character, or person related to the topic being studied. Encourage the children to be sensitive to the person's or object's needs and feelings in their responses.

2 - 8

6. Poetry Plus

Challenge children to make a class collection of poems about people, feelings, and needs. Poems like Shel Silverstein's "Hug of War" and Eloise Greenfield's "By Myself" are good examples of individual poems. Poetry collections of Carl Sandburg, Langston Hughes, and Robert Frost are sources of more sophisticated examples for older students.

3 - 8

7. Yesterday, Today, and Tomorrow

Have children analyze themselves across time by writing a Yesterday, Today, and Tomorrow poem. Prompt them to consider how feelings, interests, and priorities might change with time.

◯	*Yesterday was...*
	Crawling, crying, hugging,
	Being too little for rides at the fair,
	Getting lost at family picnics,
	Wishing I was old enough to cross the street.
	Today is...
	Running, learning, growing,
◯	*Riding all the rides at the fair and getting sick,*
	Taking my friends to our family picnic,
	Wishing I was old enough to stay up late.
	Tomorrow may be...
	Driving, working, smiling,
	Watching my kids ride at the fair,
	Celebrating how large our family has become,
◯	*Wishing for a happy, productive life for us all.*
	Louis, 7th grade

4 - 8

8. Human Issues

Brainstorm with your class significant human problems confronting students today. Reach consensus on the six that are most important. Then, establish criteria, and rank the six with "1" being the most significant problem and "6" being the least significant on the list.

Kingore, B. (2001). <u>The Kingore Observation Inventory (KOI)</u>. 2nd ed. Austin: Professional Associates Publishing.

I do not like _____

I want to be _____

_____

I wish _____

_____

I do not want to be _____

_____

_____

_____

_____

I feel _____

_____

_____

I am not very good at

I like _____

_____

_____

I am good at _____

I am _____

_____

_____

_____

I am _____

_____

_____

_____

Kingore, B. (2001). The Kingore Observation Inventory (KOI). 2nd ed. Austin: Professional Associates Publishing.

We do not like _____

We want to be _____

We wish _____

We do not want to be __
_____
_____
_____
_____
_____

We feel _____

We are not good at

We like _____
_____
_____

We are good at

We are _____
_____
_____
_____

We are _____
_____
_____
_____

Kingore, B. (2001). <u>The Kingore Observation Inventory (KOI)</u>. 2nd ed. Austin: Professional Associates Publishing.

Thinking about _____
OBJECT or PERSON

Thinks about:_____   **Sees:** _____
_____   _____
_____   _____

Hears: _____   **Smells:** _____
_____   _____
_____   _____

ILLUSTRATION

[illustration box]

Says: _____   **Touches:** _____
_____   _____
_____   _____

Tastes: _____   **Cares about:**_____
_____   _____
_____   _____

Would like to be: _____
_____
_____
_____

Kingore, B. (2001). The Kingore Observation Inventory (KOI). 2nd ed. Austin: Professional Associates Publishing.

Grades	*ACCELERATED LEARNING*

K - 2

1. Attributes Analysis

Have students use attribute blocks to demonstrate and explain 10 ways to categorize. Notice how many different attributes and the complexity of the attributes children include in each categorization. Advanced learners simultaneously categorize by multiple, more complex attributes.

K - 4

2. Game Logic

Have children work individually or in small groups to determine ways to validate or disprove that the person who goes first in a game has a better chance of winning. Ask students to organize their information and share it with the class orally, in written form, or through graphics

> ## The formulation of a problem is often more essential than its solution.
> Albert Einstein

K - 5

3. Process Analysis

As a writing and thinking activity, ask children to list the sequence for doing a task such as making a bed, walking the dog, drawing a silhouette, or completing a science experiment. Then, they leave off the title, omit one step of the process, and challenge others to identify the process and replace the missing step.

K - 8

4. Codes and Code Writing

Students assemble a class or individual collection of codes. Then, they write and exchange increasingly complex coded messages relating to the content being studied. Students who are interested can research the use of codes during World War II and investigate how certain Native American languages were used for codes.

Lindsay

1. Take the piloe off.
2.
3. Put the piloe back on.
4. Pule the quilete on the piloe.
5. Tuk the quilete under the piloe.

Kingore, B. (2001). <u>The Kingore Observation Inventory (KOI)</u>. 2nd ed. Austin: Professional Associates Publishing.

2 - 5

5. The Beginnings of Writing

Encourage students to investigate early writing forms such as pictographs and hieroglyphics. What might be inferred about the culture from its type of writing and writing materials?

2 - 8

6. Math Process Letters

Have students choose real or fictitious, well-known characters. They then write a letter to that character explaining how to work a challenging math problem. Writing a clear and effective process explanation challenges students to demonstrate their mastery of a process without continuing with additional problems to compute.

$$215 \overline{)\ 1210}$$

Dear Edgar Poe,

Your interest in my homework may be sincerely minute, but you might find interest in this particular problem.

To solve the problem, you must divide 1210 by 215. When you do, the answer is 5, but it does not go evenly and you end with a remainder. However, we are not working this problem with remainders, so the next step is to add zeros behind the decimal place on 1210 until you get an exact answer. Some problems do not have an exact answer, and the decimals go on forever sometimes. But, this answer is exact to the 1 millionth decimal place. The actual answer is: 5.627907.

This problem wasn't too bad, but in the future I would suggest avoiding long division.

Sincerely,
Scott

2 - 8

7. Math Error Analysis

The students write an error analysis for one or two mistakes they made in computation. One or two answers are marked wrong by the teacher. The student then has to determine each error and write two sentences that answer the following questions:

1. What is incorrect in this problem?
2. How can the error be corrected?

My answer was wrong because I put the decimal point in the wrong place, and that messed up my subtraction. When I copy the problem, I need to be careful to line up the decimal points in each part of the problem.

3 - 8

8. Factorials

Have students read <u>Anno's Mysterious Multiplying Jar</u> by Masaichiro and Mitsumasa Anno, and discuss the amazing numerical happenings. Then, students write and illustrate a book to explain another mathematical concept.

Kingore, B. (2001). <u>The Kingore Observation Inventory (KOI)</u>. 2nd ed. Austin: Professional Associates Publishing.

3 - 8

9. **PMI, PMIQ, and PMIV**

PMI is a critical thinking strategy developed by Edward deBono. DeBono (1993) describes the basis of his strategy as helping make an effort to find the advantages (P=Plus), the disadvantages (M=Minus) and the interesting points (I=Interesting) about an idea.

The PMI strategy is easily implemented by folding plain paper in thirds to create areas for organizing PMI responses. However, a blank PMI form is also provided in this section that may be used to prompt evaluation of the material read in science, social studies, math, or language arts. For example, intermediate and middle school students have effectively used the format to analyze historical events and characters by writing two or three sentences about the content in each section. The form is also used by teachers to create an overhead transparency on which to model the strategy with students. It is designed horizontally for handwriting ease.

Consider varying deBono's original strategy to better focus content analysis. For example, I used PMIQ and added a questioning component (Q=Question) to prompt students to pose an interesting question, to address an unknown, or to discuss a confusing point. Another variation I found applicable is PMIV that includes a concentration on the language of the discipline (V=Vocabulary) and challenges students to move from generalities to the more specific words of a scientist, mathematician, historian, or author.

PMI

TOPIC: *Eukaryotic cells in humans*

PLUS   *Eukaryotic cells build the human body.*
They reproduce themselves so the body can grow and repair itself.
Different kinds of cells are specialized to do different things like muscle cells, blood cells, and brain cells.
White blood cells in the immune system defend the other cells.

MINUS   *Cells are fragile and can be easily damaged or become cancerous.*
Viruses infect eukaryotic cells and make the cell reproduce the virus.
All cells need a specific environment to live.

INTERESTING   *Cells in the brain can tell cells in a toe what to do.*
A eukaryotic cell has its DNA in a nuclear membrane, but a prokaryotic cell doesn't.
A eukaryotic cell is like a little human with little organs called organelles, a brain which is the nucleus, and an outer skin called the membrane.
It would be interesting if humans could cooperate as efficiently as their cells.

Strategy adapted from: Edward deBono
CoRT Thinking Model

Kingore, B. (2001). The Kingore Observation Inventory (KOI). 2nd ed. Austin, TX: Professional Associates Publishing.

Kingore, B. (2001). The Kingore Observation Inventory (KOI). 2nd ed. Austin: Professional Associates Publishing.

PMI

TOPIC: _____

PLUS

MINUS

INTERESTING

Strategy adapted from: Edward deBono
CoRT Thinking Model

Kingore, B. (2001). The Kingore Observation Inventory (KOI). 2nd ed. Austin, TX: Professional Associates Publishing.

CHAPTER 7
Literature Activities to
Encourage High-level Responses

Quality literature and the nurturing activities teachers do so well and love to use can also serve to assess gifted potential and increase our appropriate responses to advanced learning needs. This section organizes numerous books according to the seven categories of the KOI. The books and activities are designed to use with all children while the teacher observes students' responses and notes behaviors characteristic of advanced learners.

Some books have connections to several or even all of the seven categories. Two books by the award-winning authors Maurice Sendak and Chris Van Allsburg are presented in the first section of this chapter as examples illustrating multiple activities for all seven KOI categories. Some activities appropriate for young students are suggested using Where the Wild Things Are; applications more appealing to older students are suggested using The Mysteries of Harris Burdick.

The remainder of the chapter consists of literature activities correlated to separate KOI categories. Each bookshelf of activities has the KOI category to which it is applied listed at the top. The complete bibliographic reference for each book is included within the annotated bibliography in Chapter 8. A blank of the activity bookshelf format is provided at the end of this chapter for you to copy and organize your own book notes and activities.

The purposes of the literature activities are to enable teachers to:
- Observe students' responses and note behaviors characteristic of advanced learners;
- Provide a variety of literature activities with which students from diverse backgrounds can personally relate and successfully complete on many different levels;
- Connect literature to a myriad of topics, content areas, and grade levels;
- Springboard discussions and more extensive topic responses;
- Celebrate diverse thinking by encouraging students to respond with multiple correct responses at different levels of understanding and interpretation;
- Replace worksheet activities that require little thinking with active participation tasks that challenge students to generate responses; and
- Assess students' interpretation, depth, and complexity of content.

Kingore, B. (2001). The Kingore Observation Inventory (KOI). 2nd ed. Austin: Professional Associates Publishing.

Activities for <u>Where The Wild Things Are</u>

Sendak, Maurice. (1963). <u>Where The Wild Things Are</u>. Illus. Maurice Sendak. New York: Harper & Row. A boy's imagination takes over when he is sent to his room. Caldecott Honor.

ADVANCED LANGUAGE

- Discuss the difference between real and imaginary things. Children fold a paper in half to draw real things on one side and imaginary on the other. Later, cut them apart for children to place on an interactive bulletin board or group poster titled "Real or Imaginary".
- Cut out large, monster-shaped paper. Brainstorm and write scary words or words to describe monsters. Post these words so children can incorporate them into creative writing experiences.
- Brainstorm words to describe the wild things in the illustrations. List the words on the board, and ask children to rank their top five favorites.
- Re-read the story. Ask children to raise their hands anytime they hear an interesting, unusual, or new word. Write each word on a chart for discussion.
- Brainstorm and list many interesting words that start with M, like Max's name. Talk about repeating phonemes, long words, short words, and the number of syllables. Let children draw pictures to illustrate the M words and tape them around the list.
- Students create analogy statements, such as: "I am like a wild thing when _____."

ANALYTICAL THINKING

- Show the cover of a book, and ask children to predict what the story is about. Write their responses on the board or chart paper. After reading, compare their predictions, and put a check by those that actually occurred.
- Ask children to listen as you read the story to find out what word the author uses repeatedly to describe the wild things. (The word is "terrible".) Discuss if the wild things in this story were really terrible and dangerous. What real wild things could be dangerous to us? List each and tell why or how they could be dangerous.
- Discuss different settings in the book: Max's bedroom, the boat, the ocean, the forrest. Brainstorm other possible settings. Develop a new event for the story: What would Max or a wild thing do in _(a new setting)_ ?
- Use the term WILD THINGS as an acrostic to organize retelling the story. Accent the sequence of the story and the most significant events.
- Brainstorm several objects in the story such as the tree, moon, ocean, suit, and boat. Children use construction paper and popsicle sticks to make one of the objects. They then hold up each appropriate prop as the story is re-read.
    VARIATION: Make the objects out of felt or Pelon™, and let the children create the story on a flannel board as the book is re-read.
- Draw and label a character map of Max.

Kingore, B. (2001). <u>The Kingore Observation Inventory (KOI)</u>. 2nd ed. Austin: Professional Associates Publishing.

MEANING MOTIVATION

- Ask students to explain why Max's supper is still hot at the end of the story.
- Students use a prediction from the pre-reading discussion of the cover and write a new story.
- Encourage individual children to write stories in books shaped as monsters, a sailboat, or a wolf suit.
- How might monsters sound if we actually heard them? Tape record children making "monster" sounds. As you read the story aloud, play the children's recording for sound effects during the wild rumpus part of the story.
- What if the wild things made Max stay? Have students complete a story map for the events that might result.
- Discuss the value of imagination.
- Address the issue of talking back to parents as Max did to his mother.

PERSPECTIVE

- Encourage children to discuss costumes they have worn, such as in a play or at Halloween. Let them role play how they might act when wearing specific costumes. Discuss why people might behave differently when wearing costumes.
- Let pairs work together to develop illustrated pages for a class big book of the story.
- Students make monster masks from paper plates with eye holes cut out. Encourage all children to think of ways to make their masks different from everyone else's. Then, have a monster parade set to music. What kind of music would be best for the parade? How should different monsters move to the music?
- Let students make wild-thing vests from paper sacks. Provide crayons or markers in vivid colors, buttons, yarn, and fabric scraps to glue on the vest. Show the children how to fringe strips of bright construction paper to glue on their vests.
- Students make wild-thing puppets using Styrofoam™ cups, popsicle sticks, pipe cleaners, foil, brads, nuts/bolts, paper clips, yarn, sequins, and related items. Act out the story.
- Students draw how a wild thing looked to Max or how Max looked to a wild thing.
- Students write what a wild thing might want to say to Max.

SENSE OF HUMOR

- Brainstorm, as a class, the unusual funny features a wild thing might have. Then, design one or more page-size versions of a funny wild thing. Enlarge the designs to 36x36 or larger. Cut out two of each. Next, children help staple the two sides together and stuff the figure with wads of newspaper. Later, hang the finished wild thing in a reading area with the book, audiotape, and sign "Hanging Out with the Wild Thing".

Hanging Out with the Wild Thing!

Kingore, B. (2001). The Kingore Observation Inventory (KOI). 2nd ed. Austin: Professional Associates Publishing.

- Let children write riddles about the events or objects in the book.
- Develop a class book titled "Funny Monsters". "The funniest thing a monster could do is _____ because _____."
- Teach students how to create a monster book of flip strips. (The procedure is described on page 100.)
- Re-read the story, and have children vote on what they think is the funniest or silliest part.
- Make up funny names for each wild thing appropriate to its appearance.

SENSITIVITY

- How did the wild things feel about Max?
- Max was sent to bed without supper, and he sent the wild things to bed without supper. How does what others do to us influence what we feel and do?
     CLASS EXPERIMENT: Have children smile at everyone in the hall. Later, frown at everyone. Discuss how people reacted to each. How does the way we feel and act influence how others feel and act toward us?
- Students finger paint an ocean scene. Let children help decide which music to play while painting. Which sounds like ocean music? Which helps you feel the way sailing on an ocean might make you feel?
- Let children write and illustrate how they think monsters might feel. "I think monsters feel _____ when _____ because _____."
- Maurice Sendak mentioned in an interview that when he was a child, he found a Mickey Mouse mask in a box of corn flakes. Why do you think that was important to him?

ACCELERATED LEARNING

- Provide Styrofoam™ blocks, straws, and paper for creating sailboats. Let children experiment to determine which design sails straightest, fastest, and furthest. Use a hair blower to provide a wind source. Which changes might make a sailboat move faster versus go farther?
- Have students classify the wild things by two or more attributes.
- Reduce and enlarge wild thing illustrations to produce four to eight different sizes for a math seriation task. Let the children place the pictures in order, largest-to-smallest and then smallest-to-largest.
- As individuals, in small groups, or as a class, create a rebus story using pictures of monsters and objects from the story.
- Let individuals create a code and use it to write the main idea or summary of the book. Later, children exchange codes and solve each other's.
- Encourage advanced readers to read other works by the author and use a graphic organizer to compare common story elements.

Kingore, B. (2001). The Kingore Observation Inventory (KOI). 2nd ed. Austin: Professional Associates Publishing.

Activities for The Mysteries of Harris Burdick

Van Allsburg, Chris. (1984). The Mysteries of Harris Burdick. Boston: Houghton Mifflin. Haunting illustrations accompanied by mysterious captions intrigue and inspire the reader to make sense of each page.

ADVANCED LANGUAGE

- Using only three-syllable or four-syllable words, write a new caption for one or more of the illustrations to make it more intriguing.
- Write a complete story for one picture.
- Write a story beginning with one picture and its caption from the book and ending with another.
- What might be written on the two pages of the book shown in "Mr. Linden's Library." What might be the title of the book?
- Write a review of The Mysteries of Harris Burdick for primary students.
- Write an editorial declaring whether or not this book will be valued as a classic by future generations.

ANALYTICAL THINKING

- Who actually created the pictures/captions/titles in this book? Decide whether Chris Van Allsburg or Harris Burdick was the creator, and demonstrate evidence to document your conclusion.
- What attributes do all of the pictures have in common?
- List all the differences you find between two pictures/titles/captions.
- Illustrate or explain one pattern you identify in this book.
- List ten or more items found in one illustration, and then, explain what might be the function of each item in a complete story.
- Select one illustration, and discuss what is implied in that picture.
- What is the function of the Introduction in this book?
- Why do you think Van Allsburg only uses shades of black and white to develop his illustrations?
- Identify several cause-and-effect relationships inferred in this book.

MEANING MOTIVATION

- Looking only at the cover, write what you think the book is about. After reading it, compare your prediction to what the book actually involved.
- Determine five thoughtful questions you would ask to solve the mystery of Harris Burdick's disappearance. To whom would you address your questions, and why did you select that source of information?

Kingore, B. (2001). The Kingore Observation Inventory (KOI). 2nd ed. Austin: Professional Associates Publishing.

- Apply the Socratic Method by creating a list of questions to ask someone that will help guide them toward understanding the illustrations in the book.
- Do you think Peter Wenders searched thoroughly for Harris Burdick? What are some of the ways he might have tried to find Harris Burdick?
- What issues does this book suggest?
- Write a journal entry for Harris Burdick in which he explains why he never returned to see Peter Wenders.

PERSPECTIVE

- Write a story to accompany one of the illustrations in this book.
- Compare stories that other students have written about the same illustration. Discuss points of view and styles.
- Sketch a picture to convey the same sense of mystery as one of the pictures in this book. Explain why you think your picture is mysterious.
- What is the source of light in each picture? What effect does the light have on what is in the picture?
- Rewrite the book's introduction from Harris Burdick's point of view.
- How would it change the effect of the book if Harris Burdick's pictures were in color? Would readers react differently? Add color to a photocopy of one picture to change its mood. Which colors result in the greatest change?

MR. LINDEN'S LIBRARY
_____

He had warned her about the book.
Now it was too late.

- You are Chris Van Allsburg, and you have the idea for this book. Explain your thoughts about creating <u>The Mysteries of Harris Burdick</u> in a series of letters to your publisher that includes your publisher's responses.
- Van Allsburg is also a sculptor. What elements of sculpting are suggested in these illustrations?

SENSE OF HUMOR

- Create humorous captions and titles for one or more pictures. Explain your thinking.
- Combine two pictures/titles/captions into one story for a humorous effect.
- Change one title to create a pun.
- Draw several pictures, complete with titles and captions, to create a sequel to the book titled <u>The Humor of Harris Burdick</u>.

Kingore, B. (2001). <u>The Kingore Observation Inventory (KOI)</u>. 2nd ed. Austin: Professional Associates Publishing.

SENSITIVITY

- Write journal entries describing the feelings of the characters at the moment depicted in one of the illustrations.
- Make a list of the main feeling each picture/title/caption evokes in you. Compare this to another student's list. Discuss similarities and differences.
- Which picture evokes the strongest emotional response? Explain why.
- Discuss the aesthetic value of this book.
- According to the introduction, Wenders published Harris Burdick's work after Burdick left and did not return. Discuss the ethics of publishing a work when the author/illustrator has disappeared.

ACCELERATED LEARNING

- What other authors use mystery to incite the imagination of the reader? How does their use of mystery compare with Van Allsburg's?
- Imagine every picture in the book takes place in the same general locale. Draw a map of this place which logically accounts for each picture.
- Many of the pictures in the book are mysterious because of the incongruities within them. What are some of the incongruities you found?
- Determine which of Van Allsburg's pictures/titles/captions is the best in the book. List the criteria for your decision to substantiate your thinking.
- New evidence has surfaced that indicates all the pictures belong in one story. Design a story board incorporating all fourteen pictures, in sequence, into one story.

"Mr. Linden's Library"   **Vanessa Harte**
                                    3rd period

Abby loved visiting Mr. Linden's house. He had the most wonderful books and smiled happily when he got to share them with someone else who loved to read. But this time, he was not smiling at the book she chose for bedtime reading. He warned her not to start that book, but it was too late. She was already captured by the story. She had to finish it.

Abby read well into the night and fell asleep with the book by her side. She woke to a tickling sensation--a vine grew out of the opened pages and curled around her body. It tugged at her and pulled her until she was sitting up in bed. Then the vine began to spell messages: "Read! You are not done with the best part. Finish me now." Frightened and fascinated, Abby followed the order. She finished the book. It really was an amazing story. It made her feel warm and satisfied. As she smiled quietly to herself, the vine patted her hand and receded.

In the morning, Abby tried to tell Mr. Linden what had happened. He chuckled that he always felt books appreciated a faithful reader. He obviously thought she had a dream.

Of course, It could have been a dream. Yet she wondered--why was a small vine cascading down the spine of another book on the same shelf? Abby knew that would be her next book choice.

Kingore, B. (2001). The Kingore Observation Inventory (KOI). 2nd ed. Austin: Professional Associates Publishing.

KOI CATEGORY: Advanced Language

Author: Base, Graeme   **Grade Levels:** K - 8
Book: Animalia
Behaviors: Uses language to teach others; verbally proficient
Activities:
1. Research how one of the less obvious items on any alphabet page relates to that letter of the alphabet, e.g., on the "A" page, is a snake that begins with "a". Explain your findings to another student.
2. List 40 or more words identifying items on each page beginning with the designated letter.
3. Organize the lists according to parts of speech.

Author: Bayer, Jane   **Grade Levels:** K - 5
Book: A My Name is Alice
Behavior: Uses multi-syllable words
Activities:
1. Create additional rhymes by adding one or more adjectives that start with the same letter such as a kind of merchandise sold, a type of animal, and/or a location.
2. Add an adverb that starts with the same letter to each sentence.
3. Create alliterative sentences that tell about each student's life and interests.

Author: Edwards, Pamela Duncan   **Grade Levels:** K - 4
Book: Some Smug Slug
Behaviors: Uses multi-syllable words; rich imagery
Activities:
1. Select a page, such as page 27, on which to insert another appropriate word beginning with "s".
2. Create alliterative adventures using other letters of the alphabet.
3. Which parts of this story are fact and which are fantasy? Research slugs to determine the facts.
4. Find the hidden "s" on each page.

Kingore, B. (2001). The Kingore Observation Inventory (KOI). 2nd ed. Austin: Professional Associates Publishing.

KOI CATEGORY: Advanced Language

Author: Fleischman, Paul   **Grade Levels:** 2 - 8
Book: <u>Joyful Noise: Poems for Two Voices</u>
Behaviors: Uses descriptive language; expresses similarities and differences
Activities:

1. Write a poem for two voices using rich, descriptive words to portray a contrasting view of a person or item.

> ### The Computer
>
> This infamous tool of technology is used to:
> create,
>   stress,
> expand,
>   isolate,
> illustrate,
>   dehumanize,
> inform,
>   pollute minds,
> and to   and to
> connect   frustrate
> people.   people.

2. Using Fleischman's poems as a model, write new poems for two voices that compare content-related topics from different points of view such as economy/ecology, national/states' rights, free speech/slander, and North/South.

Author: Levitt, Paul; Burger, Douglas;   **Grade Levels:** 4 - 8
           & Guralnick, Elissa
Book: <u>The Weighty Word Book</u>
Behaviors: Uses similes, metaphors, or analogies; verbally proficient.
Activities:

1. Determine other significant words used by people with expanded vocabularies. Individually or in pairs, employ metaphorical language to write scenarios for these additional words.
2. Use selected words from college-preparation vocabulary lists as prompts for scenarios.

Kingore, B. (2001). <u>The Kingore Observation Inventory (KOI)</u>. 2nd ed. Austin: Professional Associates Publishing.

KOI CATEGORY: Advanced Language

Author: Ryan, Pam   **Grade Levels:** K - 3
Book: A Pinky Is a Baby Mouse: And Other Baby Animal Names
Behaviors: Uses multi-syllable words; descriptive
Activity:

For another topic besides baby animals, brainstorm words beginning with each letter of the alphabet. Insects, dinosaurs, and rainforest life are examples of topics that work well for most letters. Then, write rhyming couplets for each. Illustrate and combine the rhymes into an alphabet book.

Author: Steig, William   **Grade Levels:** K - 4
Book: Sylvester and the Magic Pebble
Behavior: Uses multi-syllable descriptions and similes
Activities:

1. Fold a paper in half to make a two-column chart. Tape a dime to the top of the left column and a dollar to the top of the column on the right. Reread the story, stopping to record words identified as $1.00 words. Explore the meaning in context, and then, determine a simpler synonym for each word to record in the dime column.

2. Expand sentences by adding $1.00 words to simple statements. Write out both the simple and expanded sentences to illustrate the effectiveness of the elaboration.

> Sylvester found a pebble.
> Amazed Sylvester discovered an extraordinary pebble.

3. Sylvester's pebble was flaming red and perfectly round like a marble. How would your special pebble look?

My pebble is _____, _____,
adjective   color
and _____ like a _____.
adjective

Kingore, B. (2001). The Kingore Observation Inventory (KOI). 2nd ed. Austin: Professional Associates Publishing.

KOI CATEGORY: Analytical Thinking

Author: Avi   **Grade Levels:** 4 - 8
Book: Nothing but the Truth: A Documentary Novel
Behaviors: Analyzing difficult concepts or issues; logical thinking
Activity:

Use this book to motivate a debate of the responsibilities of free speech for individuals and the media. Divide into teams to research information, quotations, and positions. Increase opportunities for more complex thinking by requiring exploration of the issue from past, present, and future perspectives.

Author: Brown, Margaret Wise   **Grade Levels:** K - 8
Book: The Important Book
Behaviors: Demonstrates complex thinking; recognizes relationships; analyzes attributes
Activity:

Read The Important Book, and use its pattern to analyze the most important attributes of a topic.

The important thing about _____
is _____.
It _____.
It _____.
It _____.
But the most important thing is _____
_____.

Teaching Without Nonsense (Kingore, 1999) includes expanded and more complex versions of this activity with examples of students' products.

Kingore, B. (2001). The Kingore Observation Inventory (KOI). 2nd ed. Austin: Professional Associates Publishing.

KOI CATEGORY: Analytical Thinking

Author: Brumbeau, Jeff   **Grade Levels:** 2 - 8
Book: The Quiltmaker's Gift
Behaviors: Demonstrates complex thinking; analyze part-to-whole relationships
Activities:
1. Analyze the diamond displaying a quilt pattern on each page to make inferences about upcoming events in the story.
2. The inside of the book jacket is a slightly enlarged copy of one of the illustrated pages containing 250 quilt patterns. How many of the patterns can you find on the page? Analyze how each pattern is incorporated into the illustration.

Author: Carlson, Nancy   **Grade Levels:** K - 2
Book: ABC I Like Me
Behaviors: Analyzes attributes; analyzes experiences
Activity:
ABC We Like Our Class. Adapt the format of the book to create a class book analyzing all the things you like about your class and school. Work together in pairs to illustrate and write the text on one page of the class book.

Author: Hoberman, Mary Ann   **Grade Levels:** K - 5
Book: A House Is a House for Me
Behaviors: Takes apart and reassembles ideas; expresses relationships
Activities:
1. Write and illustrate additional analogies: A __ is a house for __.
2. Make a book using a pattern similar to the one in Hoberman's book. Think of a different relationship, and write examples for it.

> A _____ is a mom for a _____.
> A _____ is a mom for a _____.
> **But, my mom is a mom for me.**

Kingore, B. (2001). The Kingore Observation Inventory (KOI). 2nd ed. Austin: Professional Associates Publishing.

KOI CATEGORY: Analytical Thinking

Author: Macaulay, David   **Grade Levels:** 4 - 8
Book: Black and White
Behaviors: Recognizes relationships between experiences or ideas; generalizes
Activities:
1. Form four groups so each group can analyze one quadrant of every page of the book and create a text for that sequence of illustrations.
2. Read Macaulay's Why the Chicken Crossed the Road. Identify the ideas, themes, objects, people, and events that occur in both books.
3. Using different photographs, write a description for each. Then, let others analyze which description matches each photograph.

Author: Sachar, Louis   **Grade Levels:** 4 - 8
Book: Holes
Behaviors: Interprets; thinks logically and complexly
Activities:
1. Analyze the development of key characters from the beginning to the end of the book. Brainstorm their traits. With zero being the lowest to five being the highest, rate the degree of those traits for each character at the story's beginning versus the end. For example, Stanley's naiveté changed from a four to a two.
2. Compare Holes to Spinelli's Maniac Magee for elements of tall tales.

Author: Shannon, George   **Grade Levels:** K - 5
Book: Tomorrow's Alphabet
Behaviors: Complex thinking; organizes ideas in a unique way
Activity:
Using a topic of study, make a classroom book using the pattern of Tomorrow's Alphabet. Brainstorm several important concepts related to that topic to help prompt your thinking. Then, choose a letter of the alphabet to write and illustrate a page of the book. For example, in Tomorrow's Thanksgiving Book, C is for stalk, tomorrow's corn.

Kingore, B. (2001). The Kingore Observation Inventory (KOI). 2nd ed. Austin: Professional Associates Publishing.

KOI CATEGORY: Meaning Motivation

Author: Baker, Jeannie   **Grade Levels:** 3 - 8
Book: Window
Behaviors: Pursues philosophical issues; generates new ideas and
solutions
Activities:
1. The author notes that by 2020 no wilderness will exist on our
   planet, except in national parks. Choose one wilderness area, and
   develop a flow chart or draw a story board to predict the changes
   during the next several years.
2. Write a persuasive letter to the President explaining your position
   regarding the issues of preserving nature versus economic growth.

Author: Barrett, Judi   **Grade Levels:** K - 3
Book: Animals Should Definitely Not Wear Clothing
Behavior: Synthesizes meaning through words and graphics
Activities:
1. Provide the following pattern: Animals should definitely not wear
   clothing because _____. Working together, create a classroom book to write and illustrate new examples.
2. In this book, Barrett makes a statement and then offers 13 reasons
   why the statement is valid. Pose another position statement. Then,
   write and illustrate 13 reasons. An example is: Second graders
   should definitely read lots of good books because _____.

Author: Campbell, Rod   **Grade Levels:** K - 3
Book: Dear Zoo
Behavior: Depth of knowledge
Activity:
   Make a book with flaps, like in Dear Zoo, with the top edge of paper
   strips glued above key words or pictures to hide the answer. Plan a
   place to visit, such as a rainforest, and think about what animals live
   in that environment.
   Then, follow the
   pattern of the book
   to complete stories.

   | I went to _____ to observe the animals. |
   | I found a _____ but it _____. |
   | I found a _____ but it _____. |
   | I found a _____. It was perfect. I _____. |

KOI CATEGORY: Meaning Motivation

Author: Deedy, Carmen Agre   **Grade Levels:** 2 - 8
Book: Agatha's Feather Bed: Not Just Another Wild Goose Story
Behaviors: Asks provocative questions; philosophical issues; in-depth information

Activities:
1. Discuss the author's message in this story and the effective use of humor to make her point.
2. Develop a Venn Diagram comparing this book to political cartoons.
3. The story accents that everything comes from something. Research one of the items pictured in the borders, and produce a flow chart to explain the process.

Author: Hoban, Tana   **Grade Levels:** K - 5
Book: Look! Look! Look!
Behaviors: Asks penetrating questions; synthesizes meaning
Activity:
This book of photographs is available in regular size or as a big book. Look at one of the pages that reveals only part of a photograph. Before turning the page to view the whole, analyze the visible attributes of the picture, and pose three things it could be. Explain what led you to that interpretation.

Author: Hutchins, Pat   **Grade Levels:** K - 3
Book: Changes, Changes
Behavior: Synthesizes meaning with words, graphics, and structures
Activities:
1. As a cooperative learning variation, second or third graders work in groups to write the text for one event in the book. Later, as a class, the groups share their work in the sequence of the story.
2. Select the same quantity and shapes of the blocks pictured in the book. Then, build a different structure using only those blocks, and dictate or write another adventure to add to the story. Photograph the structure to post with the story.

Kingore, B. (2001). The Kingore Observation Inventory (KOI). 2nd ed. Austin: Professional Associates Publishing.

KOI CATEGORY: Meaning Motivation

Author: Jones, Charlotte Foltz   **Grade Levels:** 4 - 8
Book: Mistakes that Worked
Behaviors: Curious; synthesizes meaning
Activities:

1. Discuss with other students the role of mistakes in learning. Read Stephen Glenn's story in Second Helping of Chicken Soup, and react to the famous research scientist's view of mistakes.
2. Research eminent people to determine the role of mistakes in their successes. Post the findings on a "Mistakes that Worked" bulletin board or poster: Thomas Edison had ___ failed experiments and ___ successful patents; Judy Blume had ___ rejections but published ___ books.

Author: Viorst, Judith   **Grade Levels:** 4 - 8
Book: If I Were in Charge of the World and Other Worries
Behaviors: Generates new ideas
Activities:

1. Create a pattern poem from the title poem. Using the prompt: "If we were in charge of education", write cooperatively with other students what you would cancel, want, and not allow.
2. Change the prompt to "If we could change the world." List all the things to change. Count syllables of the listed words, and then, insert words into the pattern that communicate the intended message but match the syllable count of Viorst's original lines.

Author: Wiesner, David   **Grade Levels:** 2 - 8
Book: Sector 7
Behaviors: Asks provocative questions; philosophical
Activities:

1. Pose five questions the boy might ask to clarify the meaning of some of the events and to guide him through his adventure.
2. Write a moral for the story that states an interpretation of the intended philosophical statement the book makes.

Kingore, B. (2001). The Kingore Observation Inventory (KOI). 2nd ed. Austin: Professional Associates Publishing.

KOI CATEGORY: Perspective

Author: Charlip, Remy   **Grade Levels:** K - 6
Book: Fortunately
Behavior: Interprets multiple perspectives
Activities:
1. Discuss the positive and negative aspects of several typical childhood experiences, such as having an older sibling or going to bed earlier on school nights. Write and illustrate on the front of a paper your viewpoints of what is fortunate about an event. On the back of the same paper, write and illustrate what is unfortunate.
2. Retell a story by analyzing the fortunate and unfortunate aspects of the characters, setting, problem, events, and solution.

Author: Dorris, Michael   **Grade Levels:** 4 - 8
Book: Morning Girl
Behaviors: Interprets another's point of view; incorporates subtle components
Activities:
1. Retell other historical events from a contrasting point of view. For example, relate a Sioux woman's perspective of the battle at the Little Big Horn.
2. Using the format of Paul Fleischman's Joyful Noise: Poems for Two Voices, write a poem relating an historical event from two different points of view.

Author: Godwin, Laura   **Grade Levels:** K - 1
Book: Little White Dog
Behaviors: Demonstrates perspective in art; adds effective components
Activities:
1. Fold colored paper in half from top to bottom. On the outside, add minimal details to suggest an animal of that color. Inside, clearly draw the whole animal.

Kingore, B. (2001). The Kingore Observation Inventory (KOI). 2nd ed. Austin: Professional Associates Publishing.

KOI CATEGORY: Perspective

Author: Jonas, Ann   **Grade Levels:** K - 6
Book: Round Trip
Behaviors: Approaches problems from unusual perspective; interprets complex graphics
Activities:
1. Place a mirror at one end of a page, and share your observations. What happens to the picture? What happens to the text? Experiment with other books. Explain the differences in the results.
2. Research other books to create a classroom collection of books with pictures that change their meaning when viewed from more than one perspective.

Author: Keller, Laurie   **Grade Levels:** 3 - 8
Book: The Scrambled States of America
Behavior: Interprets patterns
Activities:
1. Relocate your state 500 miles from its present position on the map. What states are now closest? What advantages and disadvantages result from the move? How would the move affect animal and plant life?
2. Relocate a country or continent, and contemplate the ramifications of that change. Relate the discussion to the continental drift.

Author: Numeroff, Laura   **Grade Levels:** K - 5
Book: What Mommies Do Best/What Daddies Do Best
Behavior: Interprets point of view and patterns, past and present
Activities:
1. Following the pattern of the book, write stories comparing what big kids versus little kids can do or what animals versus people can do.
2. For social studies, write and illustrate a book comparing events and behaviors in two different countries or comparing the same location in two different time periods. Though the illustrations for each differ, the text for each is the same. Discuss what is similar for people regardless of location and time.

Kingore, B. (2001). The Kingore Observation Inventory (KOI). 2nd ed. Austin: Professional Associates Publishing.

KOI CATEGORY: Perspective

Author: Say, Allen   **Grade Levels:** 3 - 8
Book: Grandfather's Journey
Behaviors: Interprets past and present; interprets patterns
Activities:
1. Create time lines of the past and present depicting the grandfather's and the boy's journeys.
2. Develop a concept map demonstrating the relationships of the theme, characters, and events in the book.
3. Discuss how this book relates to people today.

Author: Shaw, Charles G.   **Grade Levels:** K - 3
Book: It Looked Like Spilt Milk
Behaviors: Demonstrates dimension or perspective in art; interprets more complex shapes
Activities:
1. Gently tear white paper into interesting shapes. Then, glue each shape on a piece of brightly colored paper, and label all four sides with what the shape looks like in that position.
2. Gently shape cotton balls, glue them on blue paper, and add details to complete the image. Complete pages for a class book using the pattern on each page: "Sometimes it looked like a ___. But it wasn't a ___."

Author: Steiner, Joan.   **Grade Levels:** K - 8
Books: Look Alikes and Look Alikes, Jr.
Behaviors: Interprets patterns and shapes; is attuned to aesthetic characteristics
Activity:
Using 8 to 15 items selected by the teacher that are included in the picture collage on one of the book's pages, determine which picture incorporates the items. (For variation, include one or two items in the box that are not on that page. Students find the appropriate picture and also determine which items do not belong.)

Kingore, B. (2001). The Kingore Observation Inventory (KOI). 2nd ed. Austin: Professional Associates Publishing.

KOI CATEGORY: Sense of Humor

Author: Choldenko, Gennifer   **Grade Levels:** K - 4
Book: Moonstruck: The True Story of the Cow Who Jumped Over the Moon
Behaviors: Catches subtle humor; responds to puns
Activity:
Use another character or a line from a nursery rhyme to create a story about the misunderstandings of that character's intentions. For example, the spider in Little Miss Muffet is actually a postal worker trying to deliver a letter. Incorporate virtuous traits in the character's actions such as determination, respect, or responsibility.

Author: Dahl, Roald   **Grade Levels:** 2 - 8
Book: Matilda
Behaviors: Catches an adult's subtle humor; interprets humor beyond agemates
Activity:
1. Discuss what Dahl's humorous story suggests about his view of contemporary adults. Who might the parents and headmistress represent in our society? What is his view of bright children? What might he suggest about their needs and nature?
2. Write and illustrate a scenario about Matilda's life as an adult.

Author: Gwynne, Fred   **Grade Levels:** 2 - 8
Book: The King Who Rained; A Little Pigeon Toad
Behavior: Uses figurative language and puns for humorous effect
Activities:
1. Draw another page for the book illustrating a different homophone, a multi-meaning word, or an example of figurative language used in a literal interpretation.
2. Compare these books to Linda Bourke's Eye Spy.

Kingore, B. (2001). The Kingore Observation Inventory (KOI). 2nd ed. Austin: Professional Associates Publishing.

KOI CATEGORY: **Sense of Humor**

Author: Lester, Helen   **Grade Levels:** K – 3
Book: Tacky the Penguin
Behaviors: Interprets humor beyond agemates; responds to puns
Activities:
1. Discuss Helen Lester's use of humor to make a serious point about valuing people. How does humor help gain acceptance of ideas?
2. Fold a paper in half from top to bottom. Draw and cut out a simple shirt connecting to the fold line. Decorate the shirt in a wild way. Then, open the shirt, and write a message inside about the value of being different.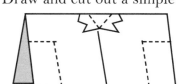

Author: Scieszka, Jon & Smith, Lane   **Grade Levels:** 2 – 8
Book: Squids Will Be Squids
Behavior: Uses humor that may seem absurd or far-out; intellectual playfulness; responds to puns
Activities:
1. Create additional fables based on contemporary interests and events. For example, write fables offering advice to peers and family.
2. Use a Venn Diagram to compare Squids Will Be Squids to Lobel's Fables. Later, complete a three-way Venn adding Aesop's fables.
3. Present one of the fables as a decision story. Write only the first two-thirds, and challenge others to write the ending and moral.

Author: Silverstein, Shel   **Grade Levels:** K – 8
Book: Falling Up
Behaviors: Uses absurd or far-out humor; uses humor to gain approval; intellectual playfulness
Activities:
1. Determine which poem in the collection is the most funny. Survey 10 students, and compile their opinions. What aspects of poems make them most funny to other students?
2. Write a poem responding to one of Silverstein's poems. Let your poem tell the rest of the story or what happens next. In your writing, incorporate the rhyming pattern and meter of the original poem.

Kingore, B. (2001). The Kingore Observation Inventory (KOI). 2nd ed. Austin: Professional Associates Publishing.

KOI CATEGORY: Sense of Humor

Author: Wood, Audrey   **Grade Levels:** 2 - 5
Book: The Bunyans
Behavior: Uses figurative language or puns for humorous effect
Activity:

Incorporate social studies information in humorous ways by writing and acting out another tale of the Bunyans. Explain their role in historical events such as how they helped the early colonists. Explain how and why they created some of the man-made wonders of the world. For example, what was their role in the building of the Eiffel Tower or the Statue of Liberty?

Author: Yolen, Jane   **Grade Levels:** K - 6
Book: Sleeping Ugly
Behavior: Catches subtle humor
Activities:

1. The story presents a sequence of funny events in which one thing leads to another. Make a sequenced paper chain in which each link contains a sentence about an event that leads to the next funny event listed on the following link.

2. Identify and list five humorous cause-and-effect relationships in this story, such as the following example.

> **Cause:** The birds and animals make their home with Plain Jane.
> **Effect:** The floors sank and the walls stank in plain Jane's house.
>
> phew!!

3. Partially overlap the faces of Plain Jane and a traditional Sleeping Beauty to create a Venn Diagram. Compare traits and events in Sleeping Ugly to a more traditional version of Sleeping Beauty.

Kingore, B. (2001). The Kingore Observation Inventory (KOI). 2nd ed. Austin: Professional Associates Publishing.

KOI CATEGORY: Sensitivity

Author: Henkes, Kevin   **Grade Levels:** K - 3
Book: Chrysanthemum
Behavior: Aware of others' needs and feelings
Activities:
1. Pretend you are a classmate of Chrysanthemum. Write or role play a dialogue with Chrysanthemum that would occur in the middle of the story as you try to help her feel more comfortable.
2. Chrysanthemum sometimes feels perfect and other times dreadful. Fold a paper in half. Write "absolutely perfect" on one half and "absolutely dreadful" on the other. Write and illustrate in each appropriate half some examples of perfect and dreadful behaviors.

Author: Krupinski, Loretta   **Grade Levels:** K - 6
Book: Best Friends
Behaviors: Bases friendships on interests; intense concern for human issues; helps promote change
Activities:
1. In which ways are children today similar to Charlotte and Lily? Draw pictures of things Lily does in the story to help Charlotte.
2. As Charlotte, write a letter to Lily to share your feelings and reactions about the doll's return.

Author: Levine, Gail   **Grade Levels:** 4 - 8
Book: Ella Enchanted
Behaviors: Expresses empathy through words and actions; high expectations; highstrung
Activities:
1. Select five commands that would best help the people of the world if the same curse in the story forced everyone to obey.
2. Create analogies to express how modern life has its own versions of "curses" that force others to obey.
              _____ is like Ella's curse because _____.
Drugs are like Ella's curse when their influence controls your actions.

Kingore, B. (2001). The Kingore Observation Inventory (KOI). 2nd ed. Austin: Professional Associates Publishing.

KOI CATEGORY: Sensitivity

Author: Polacco, Patricia   **Grade Levels:** 3 - 6
Book: Chicken Sunday
Behaviors: Is insightful of others' needs and feelings; expresses
empathic statements through words or art
Activity:
Read only the beginning of the story, but stop when the children
are accused of throwing eggs and they tell the grandmother they
did not do it. Determine the most thoughtful solution for all concerned. Then, finish reading the story, and compare your ideas to
the author's solution.

Author: Polacco, Patricia   **Grade Levels:** 4 - 8
Book: Pink and Say
Behaviors: Expresses empathic statements through words or art;
interprets behaviors
Activity:
Develop an acrostic using the title of the book. For each letter,
organize significant feelings, events, theme, and character traits
based on the story.

Passed out in a blood-soaked pasture,
Injured, fever-dreaming--another war victim.
Now, strong mahogany hands pull me up:
"**K**eep movin', or marauders will catch us."

Across fields and gullies, he pulls me, carries me.
Never feeling safe until I wake in her warmth,
Doesn't judge me any different than her own child.

Scared! A deserter. Have to go back?
A bullet takes her; a noose for him.
Yet their memory lasts in me and the hand that touched
        Lincoln's hand.

Kingore, B. (2001). The Kingore Observation Inventory (KOI). 2nd ed. Austin: Professional Associates Publishing.

KOI CATEGORY: Sensitivity

Author: Rankin, Laura   **Grade Levels:** K - 4
Book: The Handmade Alphabet
Behaviors: Displays concern for human issues; expresses empathy through words or art
Activities:
1. Learn the sign language alphabet. Sign to others a message of friendship.
2. Research the origin of sign language.
3. Interview special education consultants and counselors at your school to learn your district's plan for students with special needs.

Author: Ringgold, Faith   **Grade Levels:** K - 6
Book: Aunt Harriet's Underground Railroad in the Sky
Behaviors: Demonstrates a strong sense of fairness and justice; seeks resolution of moral dilemmas
Activities:
1. Write a letter to Harriet Tubman in which you express your feelings and reactions to her life's work.
2. Make a list of five people you would like to meet who lived at the same time as Harriet Tubman. What would you want to learn from each?
3. Analyze the illustrations in the book. Select an appropriate art media to use, and make a picture to add to this book.

Author: Van Allsburgh, Chris   **Grade Levels:** K - 6
Book: Just a Dream
Behaviors: Insightful of needs; expresses empathic statements
Activity:
The boy's dream continues as he visits where you live. Write and illustrate another episode for the book involving an environmental concern in your area.

Kingore, B. (2001). The Kingore Observation Inventory (KOI). 2nd ed. Austin: Professional Associates Publishing.

KOI CATEGORY: Accelerated Learning

Author: Cole, Henry   **Grade Levels:** K - 3
Book: I Took a Walk
Behaviors: Demonstrates an unexpected mastery of complex science concepts; categorizes; observant of relationships
Activity:
(Provide a community journal for scientific observations. Place a spiral notebook close to a window or an area near a classroom animal.) Record your name, date, and observations about the plant and animal life. Respond to other students' observations orally or by writing in the journal.

Author: Freedman, Russell   **Grade Levels:** 4 - 8
Book: Lincoln: A Photobiography
Behaviors: Comprehends advanced ideas, concepts, and implications; uses a variety of tools to access information
Activities:
1. Only a few personal items were found on Abraham Lincoln's body when he died. Interpret what each of these items suggests about his character, values, and needs.
2. Analyze the traits of leadership demonstrated by Lincoln. Then, use multi-media resources to access information about a modern president, and compare that person's traits of leadership to Lincoln's.

Author: Heller, Ruth   **Grade Levels:** K - 5
Book: Chickens Aren't the Only Ones
Activity:
Develop an ABC list by writing an example of an oviparous animal for each letter of the alphabet. Vary the task by writing sentences about oviparous animals that begin with each letter of the alphabet.

Kingore, B. (2001). The Kingore Observation Inventory (KOI). 2nd ed. Austin: Professional Associates Publishing.

KOI CATEGORY: Accelerated Learning

Author: Schwartz, David M.   **Grade Levels:** 3 - 8
Book: How Much Is a Million?
Behaviors: Comprehends advanced ideas, concepts, and implications; accesses information with ease using an unexpected variety of tools
Activities:
1. Compute the average height of the class. What would be the total height of a column of one million students of that height?
2. Research the heights of the tallest building in the world, the tallest mountain, and the altitude at which planes fly. Compare your calculations from Activity 1 to these heights. What do you conclude?

Author: Schwartz, David M.   **Grade Levels:** K - 8
Book: If You Hopped Like a Frog
Behaviors: Comprehends advanced ideas, concepts, and implications; categories by multiple, often less-obvious attributes
Activities:
1. Develop and illustrate a different ratio. Research another animal, and write a factual statement comparing its attributes to human ones. Then, write a paragraph explaining your facts.
2. Create analogies comparing different human and animal attributes. For example, a toddler is like a hummingbird when it _____ and _____.

Author: Tompert, Ann   **Grade Levels:** K - 8
Book: Grandfather Tang's Story
Behaviors: Comprehends advanced ideas and concepts; creates advanced products
Activities:
1. Use paper or felt copies of the seven tans to create the fairy fox figures as the story proceeds. Then, create an original figure, and tell another story of the foxes' adventures.
2. Arrange all seven tans to make the first letter of your name. Try to make each letter of the alphabet.
3. Research the Chinese folk lore regarding the fairy foxes.

Kingore, B. (2001). The Kingore Observation Inventory (KOI). 2nd ed. Austin: Professional Associates Publishing.

KOI CATEGORY:

Author: **Grade Levels:**
Book:
Behaviors:
Activities:

Author: **Grade Levels:**
Book:
Behaviors:
Activities:

Author: **Grade Levels:**
Book:
Behaviors:
Activities:

Kingore, B. (2001). The Kingore Observation Inventory (KOI). 2nd ed. Austin: Professional Associates Publishing.

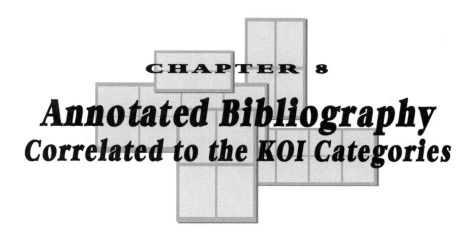

CHAPTER 8
Annotated Bibliography
Correlated to the KOI Categories

Quality literature is a vital component in an environment that nurtures talents. It is certainly developmentally appropriate to share excellent books with children of all ages. This annotated bibliography of exceptional children's books is organized according to the primary KOI category each book represents. When a book is listed under one category, it does not mean that the book is effective only for that category. Indeed, quality literature provides multiple learning opportunities through the creative applications planned by experienced teachers. The categorization signifies that the book has been particularly effective eliciting behaviors in that category. Because quality literature has many application possibilities, most of these books also involve other categories. The determining factor is the behavior(s) a teacher intends to elicit.

This bibliography includes some favorite children's literature appropriate for kindergarten through eighth grade. The titles are a balance of newer and older books. The newer works provide opportunities to continually enlarge the quantity of books used instructionally while the older books extend teaching connections with great proven books that are readily available in most libraries. While most of the books are in print, a few out of print titles are included that are worth looking for in your library. Grade level spans are listed for each book as most great books can and should be used by multiple grade levels to allow students to revisit favorites and benefit from the increased insights they develop with age. The annotation indicates if the book won a Caldecott or Newbery award or honor because students love to know the special recognitions a book receives.

> *The more you read, the better you get at it;*
> *the better you get at it, the more you like it;*
> *and the more you like it, the more you do it.*
> *The more you read, the more you know;*
> *and the more you know, the smarter you grow.*
>
> JIM TRELEASE

Kingore, B. (2001). The Kingore Observation Inventory (KOI). 2nd ed. Austin: Professional Associates Publishing.

Think about these ideas as you select the most appropriate titles from the bibliography to complement your instruction.

- Preread any book you are considering, and be sensitive to possible objections in some stories. Something as innocent as a child's name used for a negative character can affect a student in your class in an unintentional way.

- It is an asset if a book relates to the instructional topics and objectives for your grade level. However, some books deserve to be shared just because they are so enjoyable.

- Endeavor to personalize this list by writing notes about results and future applications each time you use a book.

- Keep reading. Librarians and media specialists are valuable assets in your continuous search for great literature. Discover new titles to add to your book lists and inspire children with your enthusiasm for reading.

- "One Hundred Books that Shaped the Century" (Breen, et.al., 2000) is a fascinating list selected by a team of literature experts as the 20th century's most significant books for children and young adults. Refer to this annotated list and compare which ones the students in your classes have read or missed. The comparison is certain to elicit extensive discussion. Many gifted readers will be intrigued finding out how many recognized books they have read and debating with others why another cherished book should have made the list.

- Determine your reading objectives for students, and use those objectives to prioritize book selections and instructional applications. The following are examples of objectives that guided other teachers.

READING OBJECTIVES FOR ADVANCED LEARNERS

Encourage students to:
- Want to read;
- Use reading as a source of enjoyment and information;
- Read widely;
- Read at appropriately challenging levels and pace;
- Analyze ethical and moral issues;
- Expand vocabulary and fluency in reading, writing, and speaking;
- Evaluate reading material for authenticity, validity, and objectivity;
- Use books to continue life-long learning; and
- Develop complex and in-depth responses to books far beyond book reports.

Kingore, B. (2001). The Kingore Observation Inventory (KOI). 2nd ed. Austin: Professional Associates Publishing.

Annotated Bibliography
Correlated to the KOI

Grades	A	Designates that a literature activity is included in Chapter 7

ADVANCED LANGUAGE

K - 1		Ahlberg, Janet & Allan. (1978). <u>Each Peach Pear Plum</u>. New York: Viking Penguin. This book incorporates a predictable "I Spy" format with familiar nursery rhyme and fairy tale characters.
K - 6		Ahlberg, Janet & Allan. (1986). <u>The Jolly Postman or Other People's Letters</u>. Boston: Little Brown. This manipulative book has envelopes and letters to fairy-tale characters, all delivered by a jolly postman.
K - 5		Barrett, Judi. (1998). <u>Things That Are Most in the World</u>. New York: Atheneum. This pattern book answers silly questions about superlatives.
K - 8	A	Base, Graeme. (1986). <u>Animalia</u>. New York: Harry N. Abrams, Inc. <u>Animalia</u> is a stunningly illustrated alphabet book with alliterative captions and intriguing details.
K - 5	A	Bayer, Jane. (1984). <u>A My Name is Alice</u>. New York: Dial. This pattern book of alliteration motivates children to create new rhymes.
K - 6		Edwards, Pamela D. (1995). <u>Four Famished Foxes and Fosdyke</u>. New York: HarperCollins. Four famished foxes frolic through a fun-filled food adventure.
K - 4	A	Edwards, Pamela Duncan. (1996). <u>Some Smug Slug</u>. New York: HarperCollins. A slug is so smug in his journey that he is unaware of the danger awaiting him at the end. This alliterative adventure has rich vocabulary and hidden elements to extend thinking.
2 - 8	A	Fleischman, Paul. (1988). <u>Joyful Noise</u>. New York: Harper & Row. This book has 14 fascinating poems told in the "voices" of insects to act out in pairs or in two groups. Newbery Medal.
3 - 8		Frasier, Debra. (2000). <u>Miss Alaineus: A Vocabulary Disaster</u>. San Diego: Harcourt Inc. This clever book uses a humorous story to motivate dictionary skills and vocabulary development.
4 - 8		Heller, Ruth. (1987). <u>A Cache of Jewels and Other Collective Nouns</u>. New York: Grosset & Dunlap. This beautifully illustrated book uses rhyme to teach collective nouns.
K - 1		Hutchins, Pat. (1968). <u>Rosie's Walk</u>. New York: Macmillan. Rosie the hen goes for a walk over, under, around, and through the barnyard. Someone is following her!
2 - 6		Hutchins, Pat. (1989). <u>Which Witch is Which?</u> New York: Greenwillow. A problem at a birthday party is posed, and clues are given. Thinking is required.

1 - 6   Johnson, Tony. (1994). <u>Amber On the Mountain</u>. New York: Puffin. Amber is isolated with her family until she befriends a girl from the city and gains determination to learn to read and write. The book is replete with similes.

3 - 8   Lester, Helen. (1997). <u>Author: A True Story</u>. Boston: Houghton Mifflin. This is a humorous but true account of becoming an author.

4 - 8 **A**   Levitt, Paul M., Burger, Douglas A., & Guralnick, Elissa S. (1985). <u>The Weighty Word Book</u>. Colorado: Bookmakers Guild. These humorous tales make complex vocabulary memorable.

K - 1   Martin, Bill. (1983). <u>Brown Bear, Brown Bear, What Do You See?</u> (1991). <u>Polar Bear, Polar Bear, What Do You See?</u> New York: Holt. These are very predictable pattern books that children "read" after just one read-aloud exposure.

K - 3   Martin, Bill & Archambault, John. (1989). <u>Chicka Chicka Boom Boom</u>. Allen, Texas: DLM. The repeating lines in this hauntingly rhythmic book march children through the alphabet.

K - 5   Numeroff, Laura Joffe. (1985). <u>If You Give a Mouse a Cookie</u>. (1989). <u>If You Give a Moose a Muffin</u>. (1998). <u>If You Give a Pig a Pancake</u>. New York: HarperCollins. These predictable circle stories, loved by children, offer effective prompts for many writing activities.

K - 3 **A**   Ryan, Pam M. (1997). <u>A Pinky Is a Baby Mouse: And Other Baby Animal Names</u>. New York: Hyperion Paperbacks for Children. The different names of baby animals are explained in rhyming verses.

K - 4 **A**   Steig, William. (1969). <u>Sylvester and the Magic Pebble</u>. New York: Simon & Schuster. Sylvester is in a predicament when he finds a magic stone and a hungry lion. This is a perfect story for illustrating loving family relationships and modeling sophisticated vocabulary. Caldecott Medal.

K - 5   Steig, William. (1986). <u>CDC!</u> (2000). <u>CDB!</u> New York: Windmill. The text in these books look like a secret code, but the puzzle is solved when the letters are read aloud.

2 - 8   Viorst, Judith. (1994). <u>Alphabet From Z to A</u>. New York: Atheneum. Rhyming verses note some anomalies in English pronunciation and spelling with beautiful illustrations.

4 - 8   Wilbur, Richard. (1997). <u>The Disappearing Alphabet</u>. San Diego: Harcourt Brace. The humorous rhymes relate the consequences when various letters of the alphabet disappear.

1 - 6   Young, Ed. (1989). <u>Lon Po Po: A Red-Riding Hood Story from China</u>. New York: Scholastic. The story of Red Riding Hood is told in a Chinese adaptation. Caldecott Medal.

ANALYTICAL THINKING

4 - 8 **A**   Avi. (1991). <u>Nothing but the Truth: A Documentary Novel</u>. New York: Avon Books. This documentary novel emerges as a witty satire of high school

politics. It invites readers to question and think about what they read and hear from the mass media. Newbery Honor.

K - 8 | Bourke, Linda. (1991). Eye Spy. San Francisco: Chronicle Books. A two-tiered guessing game puzzles the reader with homophone and multi-meaning word clues for what follows on the next page.

K - 8 | A | Brown, Margaret Wise. (1999; 1949). The Important Book. New York: HarperCollins. This classic book establishes a pattern for analyzing the attributes of a whole.

2 - 8 | A | Brumbeau, Jeff. (2000). The Quiltmaker's Gift. Dublin, MN: Pfeifer-Hamilton. With stunning illustrations, this book tells the story of a king learning the true meaning of happiness. Subtle messages and intriguing substories are embedded for the discriminating reader to analyze.

K - 3 | Carle, Eric. (1969). The Very Hungry Caterpillar. New York: Philomel. A little caterpillar eats his way through the book to become a butterfly and provide an introduction to metamorphosis.

K - 2 | A | Carlson, Nancy. (1997). ABC I Like Me. New York: Viking Penguin. This feel-good-about-me book invites children to analyze their strengths.

2 - 5 | Christensen, Bonnie. (1997). Rebus Riot. New York: Dial Books for Young Readers. These rhyming verses have some words replaced with illustrations so readers must analyze the picture-text relationships.

K - 3 | Elting, Mary & Folsom, Michael. (1980). Q is for Duck: An Alphabet Guessing Game. New York: Clarion. This fun book requires children to figure out the relationship between the letter and the noun. Q is for duck because a duck quacks.

K - 3 | Griff. (2000). Shark-Mad Stanley. New York: Hyperion Books for Children. With humorous illustrations, Stanley shares numerous facts as he compares his pet goldfish to a shark.

K - 5 | A | Hoberman, Mary Ann. (1982). A House is a House for Me. New York: Puffin. This book poses analogies to houses: "A book is a house for a story."

3 - 8 | Juster, Norton. (1961). The Phantom Tollbooth. New York: Random House. This is a thought-provoking mystery told in rich vocabulary.

4 - 8 | Konigsburg, E. L. (1967). From the Mixed-Up Files of Mrs. Basil E. Frankweiler. New York: Atheneum. A sister and a brother run away from home to hide in the Metropolitan Museum of Art in New York City and decipher the mystery of a statue. Newbery Medal.

4 - 8 | Konigsburg, E. L. (1996). The View from Saturday. New York: Scholastic Inc. Four gifted students and their teacher form a team for the Academic Bowl and enhance their humanity in the process. The author's unusual writing style requires the reader to continuously analyze and infer. Newbery Medal.

3 - 8 | Lobel, Arnold. (1980). Fables. New York: Harper Row. Short, one page fables feature a variety of animal characters and worthy morals. Caldecott Medal.

4 - 8	Lowry, Lois. (1993). <u>The Giver</u>. New York: Bantam Doubleday Dell Books. This complex novel relates the story of a perfect world with no problems, fears, or pain. The Giver holds the memories of the pain and pleasure of life for the rest of the population. Newbery Medal.
4 - 8 **A**	Macaulay, David. (1990). <u>Black and White</u>. Boston: Houghton Mifflin. Macaulay presents a complex tale told in four simultaneous sequences. Caldecott Medal.
K - 3	McGuire, Richard. (1994). <u>Night Becomes Day</u>. New York: Viking. Simple pictures and matching text help children predict what comes next.
3 - 8	Paulsen, Gary. (1996). <u>Brian's Winter</u>. New York: Scholastic. (1987). <u>Hatchet</u>. New York: Trumpet. When the plane crashes, Brian is the sole survivor and must solve survival problems. Newbery Honor.
4 - 8	Raskin, Ellen. (1978). <u>The Westing Game</u>. New York: Avon. This mystery challenges the reader to follow multiple characters and plot lines to reach a solution. Newbery Medal.
4 - 8 **A**	Sachar, Louis. (1998). <u>Holes</u>. New York: Farrar, Straus, & Giroux. This intriguing, beautifully crafted novel is both serious and funny as it tells about Stanley Yelnats, a strange family history, a treasure, and finding a sense of yourself. Newbery Medal.
K - 8	Sandved, Kjell B. (1996). <u>The Butterfly Alphabet</u>. New York: Scholastic Inc. Accompanied with a rhyming couplet, every letter of the alphabet is hidden within the wings of different varieties of butterflies. The reader is challenged to analyze the whole from the part.
K - 5 **A**	Shannon, George. (1996). <u>Tomorrow's Alphabet</u>. New York: Greenwillow Books. A thinking-kids alphabet book, it contains many challenges. The children need to have alphabetic knowledge to benefit the most.
4 - 8	Spinelli, Jerry. (1990). <u>Maniac Magee</u>. Boston: Little, Brown. This parable-like story deals with racism and ignorance through an orphan boy's search for a home.
K - 3	Stoll, Ellen. (1995). <u>Mouse Paint</u>. Orlando, FL: Harcourt Brace. Three white mice outsmart a cat by walking through different primary colors, mixing them as they go. The text promotes color investigations.
2 - 8	Van Allsburg, Chris. (1991). <u>The Wretched Stone</u>. Boston: Houghton Mifflin. Men's lives change and a ship is lost in this metaphorical comment on our society. Determine what is the wretched stone, and challenge students to analyze other wretched stones in the world.
4 - 8	Wick, Walter. (1998). <u>Walter Wick's Optical Tricks</u>. New York: Scholastic Inc. Curious optical illusions tantalize the reader into analyzing what is seen versus perceived in the impossible photographs.
4 - 8	Wynne-Jones, Tim. (1995). <u>The Maestro</u>. New York: Orchard Books. Burl's life is changed in one day when he runs away from his abusive father and stumbles upon an eccentric genius living in a remote cabin.

Kingore, B. (2001). <u>The Kingore Observation Inventory (KOI)</u>. 2nd ed. Austin: Professional Associates Publishing.

MEANING MOTIVATION

3 - 8 | A Baker, Jeannie. (1991). <u>Window</u>. New York: Greenwillow. In this thought-provoking wordless book, the changing of the world's ecology is seen through a window and paralleled with the growth of the next human generation.

K - 8 | A Barrett, Judi. (1970). <u>Animals Should Definitely Not Wear Clothing</u>. New York: Atheneum. Humorous illustrations fantasize the problems animals would have with clothes. With older students, the pattern becomes a format for substantiation.

2 - 8 Bradby, Marie. (1995). <u>More Than Anything Else</u>. New York: Orchard Books. A young African-American boy dreams of learning to read. His quest is an inspiring story, especially when the last page reveals that the boy is Booker T. Washington.

K - 3 | A Campbell, Rod. (1982). <u>Dear Zoo</u>. New York: Viking Penguin. What do you get when you write the zoo for a pet? Lift the flap, and find out.

K - 4 Charlip, Remy & Joyner, Jerry. (1975). <u>Thirteen</u>. New York: Parents' Magazine Press. Multiple plots make this seemingly simple wordless book complex. Invite students to write their interpretations of one of the plots.

K - 5 Cherry, Lynne. (1990). <u>The Great Kapok Tree</u>. San Diego: Harcourt Brace. Falling asleep under the Kapok tree that he came to cut down, a man is visited by animals convincing him about the importance of the rain forest.

2 - 8 | A Deedy, Carmen A. (1991). <u>Agatha's Feather Bed: Not Just Another Wild Goose Story</u>. Atlanta: Peachtree. This is a humorous morality story filled with puns and word play.

K - 3 DePaola, Tomie. (1978). <u>Pancakes for Breakfast</u>. Orlando: Harcourt Brace Jovanovick. This wordless book uses whimsical illustrations to share a humorous story of one woman's problems getting pancakes for her breakfast. It presents great opportunities for sequencing and problem solving.

K - 4 Fox, Mem. (1985). <u>Wilford Gordon McDonald Partridge</u>. New York: Kane/Miller. Wilford's favorite friend at the retirement home loses her memory, and he wants to figure out how to find it for her.

K - 3 Guarino, Deborah. (1989). <u>Is Your Mama a Llama?</u> New York: Scholastic. A young llama asks his friends about their mothers and discovers animal differences in rhyme.

K - 5 | A Hoban, Tana. (1989). <u>Look! Look! Look!</u> New York: Greenwillow. Seeing only part of a photograph, the reader questions what the whole might be.

K - 3 | A Hutchins, Pat. (1987). <u>Changes, Changes</u>. New York: Aladdin. Wooden people rebuild structures to accommodate challenges and solve problems in this wordless picture book.

4 - 8 | A Jones, Charlotte Foltz. (1991). <u>Mistakes that Worked</u>. New York: Doubleday. This non-fiction work present the stories behind forty familiar inventions that were accidents.

K - 8   Lustig, Michael & Esther. (1994). <u>Willy Whyner, Cloud Designer</u>. New York: Four Winds Press. No one pays attention to Willy until he discovers how to create clouds in any shape. Then, his invention goes out of control, and he must solve the problem of over-clouding. Encourage students to compare it to Wiesner's <u>Sector 7</u>.

4 - 8   Macaulay, David. (1979). <u>Motel of the Mysteries</u>. Boston: Houghton Mifflin. An archaeologist discovers ruins of the ancient civilization of USA and contemplates the purpose of the Motel. Discuss how schema influences our conclusions.

2 - 6   Macaulay, David. (1987). <u>Why the Chicken Crossed the Road</u>. Boston: Houghton Mifflin. A wild series of events is set off by a chicken crossing the road. Discuss the possible consequences of seemingly unimportant occurences.

K - 5   Perry, Sarah. (1995). <u>If</u>. Venice, CA: Children's Library Press. Humorous, imaginary possibilities such as mice for hair, a moon that's square, and leaves of fish are beautifully illustrated in this book of dreams. What would it look like if...?

K - 6   Plourde, Lynn. (1999). <u>Wild Child</u>. New York: Simon & Schuster. Mother Earth gently guides her wild child to bed, but who is "Wild Child"? The colorful illustrations are astounding.

K - 3   Rathmann, Peggy. (1994). <u>Good Night, Gorilla</u>. New York: G.P. Putnam's Sons. In this humorous wordless book, a gorilla unlocks the zoo cages at night so the animals can sleep with the zookeeper.

3 - 8   Van Allsburg, Chris. (1984). <u>The Mysteries of Harris Burdick</u>. Boston: Houghton Mifflin. Haunting illustrations accompanied by mysterious captions intrigue the reader to make sense of each page.

2 - 8   **A**   Viorst, Judith. (1981). <u>If I Were in Charge of the World and Other Worries</u>. New York: Atheneum. This collection of humorous poems invites enjoyment and motivates philosophical thinking.

3 - 6   Ward, Lynd. (1973). <u>The Silver Pony</u>. Boston: Houghton Mifflin. This is a wordless book of a lonely boy's imagined interactions with a pony. Discuss the possible parallel to chat rooms on the internet where friendships are made without people meeting.

K - 6   Wiesner, David. (1988). <u>Free Fall</u>. New York: Lothrop, Lee, & Shepard. A young boy embarks on an adventure of fantasy with unusual characters and locales where anything can happen. Caldecott Honor.

2 - 8   **A**   Wiesner, David. (1999). <u>Sector 7</u>. New York: Clarion Books. While on the observation deck of the Empire State Building during a field trip, a boy is lifted away by a friendly cloud who carries him to Cloud Dispatch Center Sector 7. Encourage students to compare it to Lustig's <u>Willy Whyner, Cloud Designer</u>. Caldecott Honor.

Kingore, B. (2001). <u>The Kingore Observation Inventory (KOI)</u>. 2nd ed. Austin: Professional Associates Publishing.

PERSPECTIVE

K - 3		Bang, Molly. (1991). <u>Yellow Ball</u>. New York: Trumpet. A boy's lost ball sets up an adventure with lots of different perspectives.
K - 6		Banyai, Istvan. (1995). <u>Zoom</u>. New York: Viking. This startling adventure presents a series of scenes from expanding vintage points that reveal things are not what they seem.
K - 4		Blume, Judy. (1974). <u>The Pain and the Great One</u>. Scarsdale, NY: Bradbury. One half of this book deals with an older sister's view of her younger brother. The second half tells the story from the brother's view of his sister.
3 - 8		Bunting, Eve. (1994). <u>Smoky Night</u>. New York: Harcourt Brace. A story of learning to value other cultures during the Los Angeles riots. Caldecott Medal.
K - 6	A	Charlip, Remy. (1964). <u>Fortunately</u>. New York: Simon & Schuster. On his way to a surprise party, Ned encounters many fortunate and unfortunate things.
4 - 8		Clouse, Nancy. (1990). <u>Puzzle Maps U.S.A</u>. New York: Henry Holt & Co. The shapes of states are rearranged into colleges of plants, animals, and things. Try this activity using countries instead of states.
K - 6		Crews, Donald. (1968). <u>Ten Black Dots</u>. New York: Greenwillow Books. This is an imaginative counting book done in rhyme and bold colors. Students can create books illustrating what can be made using different numbers of dots.
4 - 8	A	Dorris, Michael. (1992). <u>Morning Girl</u>. New York: Trumpet Club, Inc. Morning Girl, a 12-year-old on a Bahamian island, shares her perspective of a ship and strangers coming to her island. The year is 1492, and the strangers are Columbus and his crew.
2 - 6		Dorros, Arthur. (1991). <u>Abuela</u>. New York: Dutton. Through a clever integration of English and Spanish, a little girl dreams about flying over New York City with her abuela (grandmother).
K - 3		Ehlert, Lois. (1988). <u>Color Zoo</u>. New York: Scholastic. Layered illustrations of simple shapes diecut from the pages change into something new with every turn. Caldecott Honor.
K - 2		Emberley, Ed. (1992). <u>Go Away, Big Green Monster!</u> New York: Scholastic. Heavy die cut pages and vivid colors allow this monster to grow and then disappear as the book is read. It is also good for sequencing applications.
K - 6		Gardner, Beau. (1980). <u>The Turn About, Think About, Look About Book</u>. New York: Lothrop, Lee, & Shephard. Each drawing is something different from all four sides of the book.
K - 1	A	Godwin, Laura. (1998). <u>Little White Dog</u>. New York: Hyperion Books for Children. Solid-colored animals are hidden, camouflaged with the background, until the light is turned on and each animal finds the next in sequence.

Kingore, B. (2001). <u>The Kingore Observation Inventory (KOI)</u>. 2nd ed. Austin: Professional Associates Publishing.

3 - 6	Gray, Nigel & Dupasquier, Philippe. (1988). <u>A Country Far Away</u>. New York: Orchard Books. Each page of this book uses simple text to explain children's daily experiences and then illustrates how that task looks in the United States versus Africa.
K - 6 **A**	Jonas, Ann. (1983). <u>Round Trip</u>. New York: Greenwillow. Read this black and white book from the beginning, turn it over, and read again. The figure/ground relationships intrigue readers.
K - 1	Joyce, William. (1985). <u>George Shrinks</u>. New York: HarperTrophy. George imagines he shrinks to the size of a mouse and has to figure out how to do everything that big people do.
3 - 8 **A**	Keller, Laurie. (1998). <u>The Scrambled States of America</u>. New York: Holt. The states become bored with their positions on the map and decide to switch places. The book incorporates interesting facts and trivia.
K - 5 **A**	Numeroff, Laura. (1998). <u>What Mommies/Daddies Do Best</u>. New York: Simon and Schuster. Creatively designed, one half of the book illustrates what mommies do best and the other, daddies. Preciously drawn animals show that mommies and daddies can do the same things.
3 - 8 **A**	Say, Allen. (1993). <u>Grandfather's Journey</u>. Boston: Houghton Mifflin Co. Torn between two countries, a Japanese-American boy recounts the similar voyage his grandfather made to America. Caldecott Honor.
K - 8	Sharmat, Marjorie Weinman. (1980). <u>Gila Monsters Meet You At the Airport</u>. New York: Viking. A New York City boy has apprehensions and preconceived ideas about moving to the West. This is an excellent book to motivate discussions of prejudice.
K - 3 **A**	Shaw, Charles G. (1947). <u>It Looked Like Spilt Milk</u>. New York: Harper Row. Children love this pattern book about cloud shapes. They can "read" it immediately!
K - 8 **A**	Steiner, Joan. (1998). <u>Look-Alikes</u>. (1999). <u>Look-Alikes Jr</u>. Boston: Little, Brown. Rhyming verses cue the reader to find the hidden items in collages of common things.
1 - 8	Striker, Susan. (1982). <u>The Anti-Coloring Book of Masterpieces</u>. New York: Henry Holt & Co. Pieces of art masterpieces are printed on a page for children to complete.
K - 3	Taback, Simms. (1999). <u>Joseph Had a Little Coat</u>. New York: Viking. This lively Yiddish tale of thrift and imagination features cutouts. Caldecott Medal.
K - 3	Thiesing, Lisa. (1998). <u>Me & You: A Mother-Daughter Album</u>. New York: Hyperion Books for Children. Black and white pictures of a mother as a little girl beside color pictures of her growing baby girl compare their childhoods.
K - 3	Turkle, Brinton. (1989). <u>Deep in the Forest</u>. Boston: Houghton Mifflin. A curious bear reeks havoc in this reverse adaptation of the Goldilocks story.

K - 8

Young, Ed. (1992). <u>Seven Blind Mice</u>. New York: Philomel. Seven mice have seven different views on what they encounter. How can they ever figure it out? Use the book with older students as a metaphor for the dangers of making judgements based upon partial data. Caldecott Honor.

SENSE OF HUMOR

2 - 6

Barrett, Judi. (1978). <u>Cloudy with a Chance of Meatballs</u>. New York: Atheneum. This is a fantasy tale about the land of Chewandswallow with good humor and prediction.

K - 5

Celsi, Teresa. (1990). <u>The Fourth Little Pig</u>. Austin, TX: Steck-Vaughn. Three little pigs have a sister who tries to convince them to overcome their fears and go outside. They have never gotten over that "big bad wolf thing".

K - 4 **A**

Choldenko, Gennifer. (1997). <u>Moonstruck: The True Story of the Cow Who Jumped Over the Moon</u>. New York: Hyperion. A determined bovine accomplishes the feat of moon jumping that only horses typically train to do.

2 - 8 **A**

Dahl, Roald. (1988). <u>Matilda</u>. New York: Viking. Matilda, a genius with selfish dolts for parents, uses her untapped mental ability to save her nice teacher, Miss Honey.

2 - 8 **A**

Gwynne, Fred. (1970). <u>The King Who Rained</u>. New York: Prentice Hall. (1988). <u>A Little Pigeon Toad</u>. New York: Simon & Schuster. These books reverse homophones and illustrate the humorous result.

K - 3

Kasza, Keiko. (1997). <u>Don't Laugh, Joe</u>. New York: G. P. Putnam's Sons. Will Mother Possum ever be able to teach her son, Joe, to play dead without laughing?

K - 3 **A**

Lester, Helen. (1988). <u>Tacky the Penguin</u>. Boston: Houghton Mifflin. Being different sometimes saves the day and lets you be a hero!

K - 6

Munsch, Robert. (1980). <u>The Paper Bag Princess</u>. Toronto, Canada: Annick Press. This humorous story is about a princess who has to outwit a dragon to save her prince.

K - 8

Noble, Trinka H. (1980). <u>The Day Jimmy's Boa Ate the Wash</u>. New York: Dial Books for Young Readers. A humorous tale of a young class on a trip to the farm. This story is an example of flashback and could be used to motivate older students to use flashback as a writing technique.

K - 4

Pilkey, Dav. (1994). <u>Dog Breath: The Horrible Trouble with Hally Tosis</u>. New York: Scholastic. Two children try to save their dog whose bad breath leads to lots of funny word plays and adventure.

K - 6

Polacco, Patricia. (1996). <u>Aunt Chip and the Great Triple Creek Dam Affair</u>. New York: Philomel Books. To protest the townspeople's love for TV, Aunt Chip has not gotten out of bed for 50 years. However, when the town forgets how to read, she must remind everyone of the power of books and teach the children to take charge of their futures.

K - 2		Raffi. (1987). <u>Down By the Bay</u>. New York: Crown. This is a favorite song in book form by a favorite performer.
K - 4		Ross, Tom. (1994). <u>Eggbert the Slightly Cracked Egg</u>. New York: G. P. Putnam's Sons. With a generous serving of puns, Eggbert has many adventures trying to fit in and be accepted.
2 - 5		Sachar, Louis. (1990). <u>Sideways Stories from Wayside School</u>. New York: Random House. Due to a construction error, Wayside School is thirty stories high, instead of one. Meet the kids that reside on the thirtieth floor.
K - 5		Scieszka, Jon. (1989). <u>The True Story of the Three Little Pigs by A. Wolf</u>. New York: Viking. The traditional tale is retold from the wolf's point of view.
K - 8		Scieszka, Jon. (1992). <u>The Stinky Cheese Man and Other Fairly Stupid Tales</u>. New York: Viking. Ridiculous and silly, these twisted fairy tales make children laugh out loud. Caldecott Honor.
2 - 8	**A**	Scieszka, Jon & Smith, Lane. (1998). <u>Squids Will Be Squids</u>. New York: Viking. This is a collection of contemporary fables with tongue-in-cheek morals.
K - 4		Siebold, Otto & Walsh, Vivian. (1997). <u>Olive, the Other Reindeer</u>. San Francisco: Chronicle Books. Olive the dog thinks he's a reindeer and goes to the North Pole to help Santa.
K - 3		Sierra, Judy. (1997). <u>Counting Crocodiles</u>. San Diego: Gulliver Books. In order to get to a banana tree on another island, a clever monkey outwits the hungry crocodiles with her ability to count.
K - 8	**A**	Silverstein, Shel. (1996). <u>Falling Up</u>. New York: HarperCollins. Silverstein creates more humorous, unforgettable characters in this collection of simple, rhyming poems.
K - 3		Small, David. (1986). <u>Imogene's Antlers</u>. New York: Crown. Imogene wakes up with a pair of antlers growing out of her head. The results are hilarious with a subtle lesson in acceptance.
2 - 5	**A**	Wood, Audrey. (1996). <u>The Bunyans</u>. New York: Blue Sky Press. In the tall tale fashion, Paul Bunyan and his family explain how they created many of the natural wonders of North America. The perspective of the art is also noteworthy.
K - 6	**A**	Yolen, Jane. (1981). <u>Sleeping Ugly</u>. New York: Coward-McCann. This twist of a traditional tale is filled with puns and justice.

SENSITIVITY

4 - 8		Abeel, Samantha. (1994). <u>Reach for the Moon</u>. Duluth, MN: Pfeifer-Hamilton. A sixteen-year-old author uses beautiful art, poetry, and prose to tell of her struggles to overcome learning disabilities and find her giftedness. Non-fiction.

Kingore, B. (2001). <u>The Kingore Observation Inventory (KOI)</u>. 2nd ed. Austin: Professional Associates Publishing.

3 - 8	Bauer, Marion D. (1986). <u>On My Honor</u>. New York: Clarion. A complex novel dealing with friendship, death, and truth. Newbery Honor.
4 - 8	Bedard, Michael. (1992). <u>Emily</u>. New York: A Doubleday Book for Young Readers. An insightful vignette of the reclusive life of Emily Dickinson is shared through a young neighbor's visit.
2 - 6	Bunting, Eve. (1996). <u>Train to Somewhere</u>. New York: Clarion. Based upon a real event, this is the story of orphan children from the East going West by train to be adopted.
K - 3	Cannon, Janell. (1993). <u>Stellaluna</u>. New York: Harcourt Brace. A baby bat accidentally lands in the nest of baby birds and begins a lesson in differences and friendship.
3 - 6	Cleary, Beverly. (1983). <u>Dear Mr. Henshaw</u>. New York: Dell. Corresponding with his favorite author helps Leigh cope with his parent's divorce and being separated from his father. Newbery Medal.
4 - 8	Curtis, Christopher P. (1999). <u>Bud, Not Buddy</u>. New York: Delacorte. This novel explores the life and hard times of a resourceful orphan in search of his father during the Depression. Newbery Medal.
2 - 6	DePaola, Tomie. (1981). <u>Now One Foot, Now the Other</u>. New York: Putnam. Bobby teaches his grandfather to walk again after a stroke, just as his grandfather had taught Bobby as a baby.
3 - 8	Fleischman, Sid. (1986). <u>The Whipping Boy</u>. New York: Greenwillow. A spoiled prince and a peasant "whipping boy" exchange places, and each learns about friendship and sacrifice. This book prompts comparisons of past and present examples of one person taking credit for another's work or being blamed for another's mistakes. Newbery Medal.
K - 3 **A**	Henkes, Kevin. (1992). <u>Chrysanthemum</u>. New York: Greenwillow. Chrysanthemum loves her name until she goes to school and is teased by her classmates. Enriched vocabulary enhances this story.
K - 4	Hoffman, Mary. (1991). <u>Amazing Grace</u>. New York: Dial. When Grace wants to try out for the role of Peter Pan, her family encourages her to be what she wants to be, but her friends are not as supportive.
K - 4	Hopkinson, Deborah. (1993). <u>Sweet Clara and the Freedom Quilt</u>. New York: Knopf. Clara discovers how to find her way to freedom and sews a quilt with a map to the North.
3 - 6	Krull, Kathleen. (1996). <u>Wilma Unlimited: How Wilma Rudolph Became the World's Fastest Woman</u>. San Diego: Harcourt Brace & Co. This is a simple but informative biography of Wilma Rudolph overcoming polio, struggling to walk, and finally becoming an Olympic runner.
K - 6 **A**	Krupinski, Loretta. (1998). <u>Best Friends</u>. New York: Hyperion. A young girl cleverly uses her doll to warn her Nez Perce friend of impending danger. The author's historical format makes this an effective model for students' historical research.

Kingore, B. (2001). <u>The Kingore Observation Inventory (KOI)</u>. 2nd ed. Austin: Professional Associates Publishing.

K - 4		Kuon, Vuthy. (1996). <u>Humpty Dumpty: After the Fall</u>. Houston: Providence. Everyone in town tries to put Humpty Dumpty back together again, but no one can help him. However, when a dove touches him, he is healed and spends his life helping others.
4 - 8	**A**	Levine, Gail C. (1997). <u>Ella Enchanted</u>. New York: Harper Collins. In this Cinderella-based novel, the spunky, intelligent heroine struggles to overcome the curse that forces her to obey any command given to her. Newbery Honor.
K - 3		Lionni, Leo. (1967). <u>Frederick</u>. New York: Random House. Frederick is different and the other mice have to learn to appreciate him. Caldecott Honor.
4 - 8		Lowry, Lois. (1989). <u>Number the Stars</u>. New York: Dell. A Jewish girl faces bravery and fear living with a family in Copenhagen during WWII. Newbery Medal.
K - 4		Martin, Bill & Archambault, John. (1987). <u>Knots on a Counting Rope</u>. New York: Scholastic. A Navajo grandfather helps his blind grandson understand blindness as a strength.
3 - 8		Mochizuki, Ken. (1993). <u>Baseball Saved Us</u>. New York: Lee & Low. This describes the terrible conditions at the internment camps during WWII and the positive focus baseball gave Japanese Americans during that time.
K - 3		Most, Bernard. (1990). <u>The Cow That Went Oink</u>. New York: Harcourt Brace. A cow oinks, and animals make fun of her until a new friend helps. This story motivates positive discussions of the value of being bilingual.
3 - 8		Naylor, Phyllis Reynolds. (1991). <u>Shiloh</u>. (1996). <u>Shiloh Season</u>. (1997). <u>Saving Shiloh</u>. New York: Dell. A series of outstanding, "kid-pleasing" books about a boy and the dog he loves. They are ideal for prompting discussions on complex issues such as animal rights, abuse, and personal ethics. Newbery Medal.
2 - 5		Parks, Rosa & Haskins, Jim. (1992). <u>Rosa Parks: My Story</u>. New York: Penguin. Rosa Parks tells her story including the incident on a Montgomery bus.
K - 2		Penn, Audrey. (1993). <u>The Kissing Hand</u>. Washington D.C.: Child Welfare League of America. Chester the raccoon does not want to go to kindergarten, but Mother comes up with a loving secret to help him.
3 - 6	**A**	Polacco, Patricia. (1992). <u>Chicken Sunday</u>. New York: Philomel. Three children get into trouble trying to buy an Easter Hat for a friend. They find a way to prove their innocence and earn money at the same time.
4 - 8	**A**	Polacco, Patricia. (1994). <u>Pink and Say</u>. New York: Philomel. Two boys, a former slave and a farm boy, suffer many injustices during the Civil War.
K - 4	**A**	Rankin, Laura. (1991). <u>The Handmade Alphabet</u>. New York: Dial Books. The author, motivated by a hearing-impaired family member, created this wordless alphabet book with each alphabet letter formed by a hand using sign language.

Kingore, B. (2001). <u>The Kingore Observation Inventory (KOI)</u>. 2nd ed. Austin: Professional Associates Publishing.

K-6	A	Ringgold, Faith. (1992). <u>Aunt Harriet's Underground Railroad in the Sky</u>. New York: Crown. Factual information and a map are included in this story of slavery and the Underground Railroad.

K-6 A Van Allsburgh, Chris. (1990). <u>Just a Dream</u>. Boston: Houghton Mifflin. An insensitive boy has a dream about the Earth's future and becomes dedicated to ecology issues.

K-5 White, E.B. (1952). <u>Charlotte's Web</u>. New York: Harper. This is the compassionate story of an emotional, naive pig who finds greatness through a spider's love. Newbery Honor.

ACCELERATED LEARNING

3-8 Anno, Masaichiro & Anno, Mitsumasa. (1983). <u>Anno's Mysterious Multiplying Jar</u>. New York: Philomel. This intriguing book illustrates the concept of factorials.

K-4 Brimner, Larry. (1999). <u>The Official M&M's Book of the Millennium</u>. Watertown, MA: Charlesbridge. In this concept book, M&M™ characters teach the history and present use of calendars and how they work--or don't work.

3-7 Cherry, Lynn. (1992). <u>A River Ran Wild</u>. New York: Harcourt Brace. This is a true story of the harmful impact pollution had on the Nashau River Valley in Massachusetts during the industrial revolution and the environmental protection that resulted from the determination of a local woman.

2-5 Clement, Rod. (1991). <u>Counting on Frank</u>. Milwaukee: Gareth Stevens Children's Books. Frank loves math and applies it to every part of his life through humorous counting, size comparison, and mathematical facts.

K-3 A Cole, Henry. (1998). <u>I Took a Walk</u>. New York: Greenwillow. This book awakens the reader to observe what nature provides--opportunities for exploration and an example of coexistence.

K-5 Cole, Joanna. (Various). <u>The Magic School Bus Series</u>. New York: Scholastic. A fun, creative way of introducing multiple scientific topics to elementary children.

4-8 A Freedman, Russell. (1987). <u>Lincoln: A Photobiography</u>. New York: Clarion. Photographs and rich text provide in-depth information about Lincoln as a person and a leader. Newbery Medal.

4-8 Freedman, Russell. (1991). <u>The Wright Brothers: How They Invented the Airplane</u>. New York: Scholastic. This non-fiction book, using historical photographs and in-depth information, explains the determination and creativity leading to Wilber and Orville Wright's invention of the airplane. Newbery Honor.

K-5 A Heller, Ruth. (1981). <u>Chickens Aren't the Only Ones</u>. New York: Grosset & Dunlap. This beautifully illustrated book uses rhyme to share interesting facts about oviparous animals. Non-fiction.

3 - 8	Lasky, Kathryn. (1995). <u>She's Wearing a Dead Bird on Her Head</u>. New York: Hyperion Books. This historical fiction personalizes the activities of the founders of the Audubon Society and the emergence of protective laws.
K - 4	Lehn, Barbara. (1998). <u>What Is a Scientist?</u> Lavern, TN: Millbrook. This book parallels the curiosity of first graders with the exploration of scientists through text and color photos.
4 - 8	Magazini, Christy. (1997). <u>Cool Math</u>. New York: Price Stern Sloan. This is a cool description of mathematics from zero to infinity with amazing math activities, math tricks, ancient puzzles, and incredible shortcuts.
K - 8	Martin, Jacqueline B. (1998). <u>Snowflake Bentley</u>. Boston: Houghton Mifflin. Persistence and family support are taught in this biography of Wilson "Snowflake" Bentley--a self-taught photographer and scientist.
K - 2	McMillan, Bruce. (1996). <u>Jelly Beans For Sale</u>. New York: Scholastic. This book is excellent for reinforcing math and money skills. The author uses photos of children, jelly beans, and coins. Non-fiction.
3 - 6	Mollol, Tololwa M. (1999). <u>My Rows and Piles of Coins</u>. New York: Clarion Books. The reader learns about Tanzanian economy and life through the story of a young boy saving to buy a bicycle. Coretta Scott King Award.
4 - 8	Morgan, Rowland. (1997). <u>In the Next Three Seconds</u>. New York: Puffin. The author uses mathematical calculations and conversions to produce tantalizing trivia predicting events in the near and distant future. He also teaches readers how to produce their own predictions.
3 - 8	Neuschwander, Cindy. (1997). <u>Sir Cumference and the First Round Table</u>. (1999). <u>Sir Cumference and the Dragon of Pi</u>. Watertown, MA: Charlesbridge. These math adventures employ the whimsical Sir Cumference to discover and explain math concepts.
4 - 8	Pallotta, Jerry & Bolster, Rob. (1999). <u>The Hershey's Fractions Book</u>. New York: Scholastic. A Hershey bar becomes a tasty, concrete lesson in fractions.
3 - 8 A	Schwartz, David M. (1985). <u>How Much Is a Million?</u> New York: Scholastic. The concept of a million become more concrete through the comparisons presented in this book.
3 - 8 A	Schwartz, David M. (1999). <u>If You Hopped Like a Frog</u>. New York: Scholastic. With hilarious comparisons of human and animal attributes, this book applies the concept of ratio and invites students to research and figure out more math relationships.
3 - 7	Sis, Peter. (1996). <u>Starry Messenger</u>. New York: Farrar, Straus, & Giroux. Galileo's own writings, maps, drawings, and timelines bring this famous mathematician, scientist, philosopher, astronomer, and physicist to life. Caldecott Honor.
K - 8 A	Tompert, Ann. (1990). <u>Grandfather Tang's Story</u>. New York: Crown. Grandfather cleverly uses tangrams to produce the fairy foxes from Chinese folklore and tell a story. Readers can tell new stories by creating additional characters or scenes with tangrams.

Kingore, B. (2001). <u>The Kingore Observation Inventory (KOI)</u>. 2nd ed. Austin: Professional Associates Publishing.

References

Anderson, R.D., Hiebert,E.H., Scott, J.A., & Wilkerson, A.G. (1985). <u>Becoming a nation of readers</u>. Washington, D.C.: National Institute of Education.

Breen, K., Fader, E., Odean, K., & Sutherland, Z. (2000). One hundred books that shaped the century. <u>School Library Journal</u>. January, 50-58.

Canfield, J. & Hansen, M.V. (1995). <u>A 2nd helping of chicken soup for the soul.</u> Deerfield Beach, Florida: Health Communications, Inc.

Ciha, T.E., et al. (1974). Parents as identifiers of giftedness, ignored but accurate. <u>Talents and Gifts</u>, 17.

Clark, B. (1997). <u>Growing up gifted</u>. 5th ed. New York: Prentice Hall.

Colangelo, N. & Davis, G.A. (Eds.). (1997). <u>Handbook of gifted education</u>, 2nd ed. Boston: Allyn & Bacon.

Davis, G. A. & Rimm, S. B. (1998). <u>Education of the gifted and talented</u>, 4th ed. Boston: Allyn & Bacon.

DeBono, E. (1993). <u>Teach your child how to think.</u> New York: Penguin Books.

Feldhusen, J.F. (1997). Educating teachers for work with talented youth. In N. Colangelo & G.A. Davis (Eds.). <u>Handbook of gifted education</u>, 2nd ed. Boston: Allyn & Bacon.

Ford, D. Y, & Harris, J. J. (1999). <u>Multicultural gifted education</u>. New York: Teachers College Press.

Greenlaw, J. .& McIntosh, M. (1988). <u>Educating the gifted: A sourcebook</u>. Chicago: American Library Association.

Jacobs, J. D. (1971). Effectiveness of teacher and parent identification of gifted children as a function of school level. <u>Psychology in the Schools</u>, 8, 140.142.

Karnes, M.B. (1983). <u>The underserved: Our young gifted children</u>. Reston, Virginia: Council for Exceptional Children.

Karnes, M.B. (1987). Bring out head start talents: Findings from the field. <u>Gifted Child Quarterly</u>, 31(4). 174-179.

Kingore, B. (1998). Seeking advanced potentials: Developmentally appropriate procedures for identification. In J.F. Smutny (Ed.). <u>The young gifted child: Potential and promise, an anthology</u>. Cresskill, NJ: Hampton Press.

Kingore, B. (1999a). <u>Assessment: Time-saving procedures for busy teachers</u>, 2nd ed. Austin: Professional Associates Publishing.

Kingore, B. (1999b). <u>Literature celebrations: Catalysts to high-level book responses</u>. Austin: Professional Associates Publishing.

Kingore, B. (1999c). <u>Teaching without nonsense: Activities to encourage high-level responses</u>. Austin: Professional Associates Publishing.

Perry, P.J. (1998). Enjoying and encouraging the young gifted child. In J.F. Smutny (Ed.). <u>The young gifted child: Potential and promise, an anthology</u>. Cresskill, NJ: Hampton Press.

Popham, W. J. (1997). What's wrong and what's right with rubrics. <u>Educational Leadership</u>, 54, 72-75.

Renzulli, J.S. (1978). What makes giftedness? Reexamining a definition. <u>Phi Delta Kappan</u>, 60. 180-184, 261.

Richert, E.S., Alvino, J.J., & McDonnel, R.C. (1982). <u>National report on identification: Assessment and recommendations for comprehensive identification of gifted and talented youth</u>. Washington, DC: U.S. Department of Education, Educational Information Resource Center.

Richert, E.S. (1997). Rampant problems and promising practices in identification. In N. Colangelo & G.A. Davis (Eds.). <u>Handbook of gifted education</u>. Boston: Allyn & Bacon.

Roedell, W.C., N.E. Jackson, and H.B. Robinson. (1980). <u>Gifted young children: Perspective on gifted and talented education</u>. New York: Teachers College Press.

Ross, P. (1993). <u>National excellence: The case for developing America's talent</u>. Washington, DC: U.S. Department of Education, Office of Educational Research and Improvement.

Slocumb, P. D. & Payne, R. K. (2000). <u>Removing the mask: Giftedness in poverty</u>. Highlands, TX: RFT Publishing.

Tittle, B. (1979). Searching for hidden treasure: Seeking the culturally different gifted child. <u>Journal for the Education of the Gifted</u>, 2. 80-93.

Torrance, E.P. (1984). <u>Torrance tests of creative thinking: Streamlined manual</u>. Bensonville, IL: Scholastic Testing Service.

Trelease, J. (1995). <u>The read aloud handbook</u>, New York: Penguin Books

Westberg, K.L., Archambault, F.X., Jr., Dobyuns, S.M., & Salvin, T.J. (1993). The classroom practices observation study. <u>Journal for the Education of the Gifted</u>, 16(2), 120-146.

Witte, R. S. (1989). <u>Statistics</u>, 3rd ed. Fort Worth: Holt, Rinehart, Winston.

Professional Associates Publications
Correlated to the Kingore Observation Inventory Categories

The following grid displays Professional Associates Publishing's activity books that have been correlated to the KOI categories of gifted potential. Depending upon the level and depth of content, the following KOI categories can be elicited when completing these activities.

	Advanced Language	Analytical Thinking	Meaning Motivation	Perspective	Sense of Humor	Sensitivity	Accelerated Learning
ENGAGING CREATIVE THINKING							
Creative Problem Solving with Literature							
Books for Creative Problem Solving	•	•	•	•	•	•	•
Elementary Example: Lon Po Po	•	•			•	•	
Secondary Example: Catherine Called Birdy	•	•	•			•	
Task 1: The Alien, Grades K-6	•	•			•	•	•
Task 2: Newspaper Bridges, Grades 1-8	•	•		•			•
Task 3: Architecture, Grades 2-12	•	•		•			•
Task 4: Golf Course, Grades 4-12	•	•		•			•
Task 5: Road Rally, Grades 4-12	•	•					•
INTEGRATING THINKING							
Increasing Thinking with Bloom's Taxonomy							
Literature	•	•	•	•	•	•	•
Math	•	•	•	•	•	•	•
Science	•	•	•	•	•	•	•
Social Studies	•	•	•	•	•	•	•
Content Puzzles	•	•	•	•			•
Relation Charts	•	•	•	•		•	•
Six Boxes	•	•	•	•	•	•	•
Automaticity Graphics	•	•					•
Fast Thoughts	•	•					•
Action Figures	•	•		•			
Venn Variations	•	•					•
LITERATURE CELEBRATIONS							
Increasing Thinking with Any Good Book	•	•	•	•	•	•	•
To Do When You're Through	•	•	•	•	•	•	•
Book Wheels	•						•
Book Making	•	•		•			•

Kingore, B. (2001). The Kingore Observation Inventory (KOI). 2nd ed. Austin: Professional Associates Publishing.

	Adv. L	An. T	M M	Persp.	S of H	Sens.	Acc. L
Graphics for Book Responses							
Ant	•	•	•	•	•	•	•
Book Map	•	•	•	•	•	•	•
Cause and Effect Map	•	•	•			•	•
Character Frame	•	•	•			•	•
Circle Map	•	•	•				•
Clip Board	•	•	•	•	•	•	•
Piggy Bank of Ideas	•	•	•	•	•	•	•
Senses	•	•		•		•	
Story Frame	•	•	•			•	
Tell It Your Way	•	•					
Literature Circles							
Self-Evaluations	•	•	•			•	
Analyzer 1	•	•					
Analyzer 2	•	•		•		•	
Discussion Director	•					•	
Illustrator		•	•	•			
Inspector	•				•	•	
Interviewer 1	•						
Interviewer 2	•	•		•		•	
Story Mapper 1	•	•					
Story Mapper 2	•	•		•			
Word Wizard	•	•					•
Readers Theater							
A Hunting We Will Go	•						
The Wind and the Sun	•						
Aesop's Fables	•	•	•				•

TEACHING WITHOUT NONSENSE

	Adv. L	An. T	M M	Persp.	S of H	Sens.	Acc. L
Comic Characters		•	•	•			
Thinking Triangle	•	•	•				•
Acrostic	•	•	•	•	•	•	•
Fact Puzzle	•	•					•
Color Logic		•		•			•
Body Rhymes	•						
Concept Map	•	•	•	•	•	•	•
I Am	•	•	•	•	•	•	•
Scavenger Hunt	•	•					•
Important Thing	•	•	•	•	•	•	•
Two-Column Chart	•	•		•			
Analysis Grid	•	•					•

Kingore, B. (2001). <u>The Kingore Observation Inventory (KOI)</u>. 2nd ed. Austin: Professional Associates Publishing.

Index

Current Publications by
Bertie Kingore, Ph.D. ——————————

Alphabetters: Thinking Adventures with the Alphabet (Task Cards)
Assessment: Time Saving Procedures for Busy Teachers, 3rd ed.
--Assessment Interactive CD-ROM
Centers in Minutes!
--Centers CD-ROM Vol. 1: Grades K-8
--Centers CD-ROM Vol. 2: Learners with Limited Reading and Writing Skills
Differentiation: Simplified, Realistic, and Effective
--DIfferentiation Interactive CD-ROM
Engaging Creative Thinking: Activities to Integrate Creative Problem Solving
Integrating Thinking: Strategies that Work!, 2nd ed.
Just What I Need! Learning Experiences to Use on Multiple Days in Multiple Ways
Literature Celebrations: Catalysts for High-Level Book Responses, 2nd ed.
Reaching All Learners: Differentiating Lessons in Mixed-Ability Classrooms
Reading Strategies for Advanced Primary Readers
Reading Strategies for Advanced Primary Readers: Professional Development Guide
Recognizing Gifted Potential: Planned Experiences with the KOI
Teaching Without Nonsense: Activities to Encourage High-Level Responses
We Care: A Curriculum for Preschool Through Kindergarten, 2nd ed.

FOR INFORMATION OR ORDERS CONTACT:
PROFESSIONAL ASSOCIATES PUBLISHING
PO Box 28056
Austin, Texas 78755-8056
Toll free phone/fax: 866-335-1460

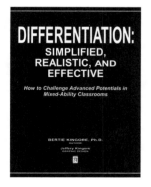

Differentiation: Simplified, Realitic, and Effective
Dr. Bertie Kingore
Grades: K - 12

Teachers want to differentiate. They certainly view it as important to their students, but they continue to experience frustration at the vastness of the task. How-to questions prevail. Management questions repeat themselves in district after district. Therefore, the focus of this book is to simplify the implementation of differentiation to increase its practice. Specific aids and examples are included because teachers found them particularly beneficial to simplify the planning and preparation process of differentiated instruction.
Over 50 reproducible figures to aid differentiation in the classroom!